*My Life
Above the Clouds*

My Life Above the Clouds

In the Footsteps of Henry David Thoreau

As Lived and Told

by
Benjamin M. Scribner
to
Margaret Rose Scribner

SANTA FE

Thanks to Steve Cagle for his assistance with the photographs in this book.

© 2015 by Benjamin M. Scribner
All Rights Reserved.

No part of this book may be reproduced in any form or by any electronic or mechanical means including information storage and retrieval systems without permission in writing from the publisher, except by a reviewer who may quote brief passages in a review.

Sunstone books may be purchased for educational, business, or sales promotional use. For information please write: Special Markets Department, Sunstone Press, P.O. Box 2321, Santa Fe, New Mexico 87504-2321.

Book and cover design › Vicki Ahl
Body typeface › ITC Benguiat Std
Printed on acid-free paper
∞
eBook 978-1-61139-358-3

Library of Congress Cataloging-in-Publication Data

Scribner, Benjamin M., 1961-
  My life above the clouds : in the footsteps of Henry David Thoreau, as lived and told / by Benjamin M. Scribner to Margaret Rose Scribner.
     pages cm
  ISBN 978-1-63293-050-7 (softcover : alk. paper)
  1. Veterans--United States--Biography. 2. Persian Gulf War, 1991--Veterans--United States. 3. Truck drivers--United States--Biography. 4. Mountain life--Idaho. 5. Thoreau, Henry David, 1817-1862--Influence. 6. Wilderness areas in literature. 7. Self-reliant living. 8. Sustainable living. I. Scribner, Margaret Rose, 1937- II. Title. III. Title: In the footsteps of Henry David Thoreau.
  PS3619.C745M9 2015
  818'.603--dc23
  [B]
                                        2014044956

WWW.SUNSTONEPRESS.COM
SUNSTONE PRESS / POST OFFICE BOX 2321 / SANTA FE, NM 87504-2321 /USA
(505) 988-4418 / ORDERS ONLY (800) 243-5644 / FAX (505) 988-1025

This book is dedicated with special thanks to my mother, Margaret Rose Scribner for making sense of all my notes and stories.

It's also dedicated to my brothers and sisters of the Armed Forces.
To those who came home, those that didn't, and to those still fighting their personal battles.

Who Is Henry David Thoreau?

As you picked up this book and began to peruse my tale, curious about its' relationship to someone named Henry David Thoreau, it was either because you already knew who he was and you might have wondered about his improbable connection to my life on a mountaintop. Well, here's the story:

Henry David Thoreau was born in 1817. He was an early environmentalist, a naturalist, an abolitionist, tax resister, essayist and leading transcendentalist. Nature was his religion. In 1845, to better communicate with the natural world, he choose to live alone in a cabin built by his own hand isolated on the shores of Walden Pond in Concord, Massachusetts on land owned by his friend and mentor, Ralph Waldo Emerson. There he observed nature, farmed, built fences, surveyed and wrote prolifically in his journal. His goal: "to live deliberately, to front only the essential facts of life, and ... learn what it had to teach." Among his better-known writings: *Walden; or, Life in the Woods* and *Civil Disobedience*. He died in 1862, at the age of 45, reportedly of tuberculosis.

I am humbled by the grandeur and forward-thinking of this man, his achievements and philosophies and buoyed by his grit and determination. His footsteps are enormous, mine are yet very small. But that I can grow, and learn, and follow in his path.

This adventure is being lived by me on the top of an Idaho mountain, but has been documented and composed by my Mom in Florida.

She is both an ardent supporter, artist, and writer.

1

> "Most men lead lives of quiet desperation
> and go to the grave with song still in them."
> —Henry David Thoreau, 1817–1862

A divorce that cruelly unearthed lies, deceit, theft, abuse of trust and power, that severs a union with a partner who blithely alienated all loved ones, all family members, a final act of separation which, for spite and spite-sake alone, dragged its opponent savagely across ten hideously pocked-marked months with idiotic wrangling, an absurd process that can, and did, empty the pockets of all but the gleeful lawyers, the outcome of which could seemingly hurl its survivor into the blackest abyss of despair or propel them, now unfettered, to the top of the highest mountain.

I landed upon a mountaintop, literally.

Growing up in the shadow of New Hampshire's magnificent White Mountain range I believed nothing could rival the glory, beauty and majesty of those beloved mountains. That is, until I discovered Idaho. Spacious skies, regal peaks, lush valleys, seemingly bottomless azure lakes and views that travel into eternity comprise the geography of this glorious state. Mankind's pitiful adjectives simply cannot justly define the awesomeness left behind eons ago by rampaging glaciers that lumbered across its surface.

Free now from the soul-eroding relationship, I needed a piece of that glory. I figured just twenty acres, far up the side of a mountain and far, far away from those who, for fifteen years, so joyfully wretched havoc upon my life would be just about right. And so with a knowledgeable lady realtor in tow, we began the rough and tumble journey traversing the rocky, twisting, old logging road several miles up into the clouds and high above the little town of St Maries.

At many of the arduous twists and turns, brief openings along the thickly forested road's edges revealed coveted glimpses into the valley below, flaunting views so splendiferous as to take our breaths away.

"We're almost there," the realtor stated. "The twenty acres I want to show you are just up ahead and ready for development. You can open up a good size clearing and build yourself a cabin. All the hunting and fishing you want will be waiting just outside your doorsteps."

"Christ! I don't want to hunt and fish there! I want to live there!" I blurted out.

The realtor looked slightly bemused and I believe I heard her eyeballs roll.

The View Took My Breath Away.

Just as we approached a broad expanse of cleared forest, courtesy of former logging operations, a patch of early morning fog lifted to reveal a view below that stunned us. The car stopped. We unfolded ourselves from its cocoon and stepped out to gaze in awe at the scene below: a valley so deep it seemed to burrow all the way to China, protectively encircled by towering mountain peaks and hovering just below our feet floated billows of misty white clouds. I thought I'd died and gone to heaven.

And then Heaven opened its door to me. For there, opposite this glorious scene, bathed in a rapturous blaze of sunshine, sat the sweetest little cabin in all of Christendom. I think I heard the Angels sing.

Then I heard the Angels Sing.

I pointed—almost stuttering—as I asked, "Who owns that?"

"Oh, the owner of this little gem is in jail and won't be coming back, so it's up for sale. However I haven't had a chance to get inside and clean it up yet. It will probably be listed next week. Unfortunately, it doesn't have the twenty acres you want, only ten."

"I don't care if it's cleaned up or not, ten acres or one. Can I have a look?"

Reluctantly, and with apologies for the disheveled state of its interior, she turned the key. We stepped inside, and at that moment I knew I'd come home.

Sweet. Absolutely sweet. Its solid green metal roof pitched skyward allowing for a second floor sleeping loft flanked by a wall of glass overlooking the mountain's highest peaks. The cabin faced north and at its ground level was a broad window reaching nearly from floor to ceiling allowing for unencumbered views of the panorama below. A front entry door, finished off in mellow pine affixed in such a way as to resemble a sunburst, added to its "road-side appeal." In fact, the cabin's entire facade boasted siding in the same mellow pine, with each board attached artfully on a 45 degree angle; an indication to me that its previous owner had cared much for this little retreat and taken great pains to create a thing of beauty on this mountainside. I wondered briefly what circumstances had ripped him from this utopia and planted him behind bars.

On the west side of the cabin was a never-finished hint of an addition covered over with a blue tarp. A probable kitchen, I thought, about 6 by 14 feet in dimension. A small picturesque wood burning pedestal-type stove occupied the corner of the cabin's "spacious" 16 by 13 foot open living space, its less-then-imposing bulk and none-too-adequate stovepipe reaching upward and out through the roof. *Humm, I wondered, would this be gutsy enough to keep me warm when the thermometer plummets and snow blankets all?* Probably not. Opposite this was a couch, several small tables and even a couple of lamps, although I detected no indication of electricity coming into the cabin. A very rustic stairway, angled first north then east, reached up and into the sleeping loft.

A very small addition, just eight by nine feet, at the cabin's rear boasted a bed, complete with bedding, and a couple more smallish side tables. On the wall behind the bed's headboard hung an Indian-style coverlet. A few sundry accessories were scattered about the tiny space. Notably the unfortunate incarcerated former owner had not had the luxury of removing his personal belongings.

I was in love.

"How soon can I buy it and when can I move in?"

The realtor immediately looked slightly taken aback. I probably represented the fastest sale she'd ever made.

The deal was an easy one. An arrangement between the realtor and the mountain developer required a miserly $300 down as a good faith deposit with a very affordable follow-up payment in a couple of weeks. From then on it would be a reasonable monthly mortgage payment. For a brief two moments I pondered this then made the quickest decision of my life.

The deal was struck.

I called my mother, far away in sunny Florida, and shouted, "Hey Ma, I'm calling you from inside my new home!"

She's a pioneer at heart and as soon as I explained the situation, she was ready to pack her bags and join me. "How soon are you going to move in?"

I was born in 1961 to hard-working parents. My dad was in the construction trade, and my mom owned a number of retail business. I was brought up believing hard work and sacrifice was the way to get ahead in the world.

I hated school, so as soon as I turned sixteen I dropped out and began work in construction, like my father. I hated that too. So at seventeen I joined the Navy. That life rather suited me. At twenty I married a seventeen-year-old girl from Mobile, Alabama. Eight years later, we divorced. By then I had retired from the Navy, and my situation was such that I suddenly became a single father to my three boys—all under the age of six. I had completed ten years of service in the Navy but had absolutely no job skills that would transfer into the civilian world. I fumbled around in several dead-end jobs, then briefly went back to school to become a commercial truck driver, and that became my life's work for the next twenty-five years.

A few years after that first divorce I married again. This time to a woman from a small Colorado town. One more son was born of that union. Then along came September 11, 2001, and with pride and patriotism I reenlisted in the Navy Reserves. Following a year-long tour in the Persian Gulf I was sent home with duel diagnoses of myopathy and neuropathy, a progressive nerve and muscle diseases that affect my hands and feet. Coupled with that my thyroid was behaving strangely. Soon after my return from the Gulf that marriage ended too.

Now I had two failed marriages behind me and faced with the of possibly of becoming a cripple. I had worked hard since age thirteen, first summer jobs, then graduating to full time. I had toiled diligently all my life to make a living for myself and my families. Now at fifty-two I had absolutely *nothing* to show for it. I was starting over from scratch.

The following tale is my account of that start-over—one of salvation, redemption and in the secular sense, one of being reborn. I began my journey into this new, challenging and exciting world, one in which I was master of my own fate, crafter of my own successes and failures, but no longer a slave to the day-to-day grind that burdens the lives of so many souls.

I'm proud to be a long-haul trucker by profession. I've been doing it for over twenty-five years, minus a two-year hiatus to serve with the U.S. Navy in Kuwait just after 9/11. As a reservist it was relatively easy, even at my age, to reenlist. However, during the time I served in the Gulf the cruel diagnosis' of myopathy and neuropathy ended my military prospects and nearly ended my truck-driving career. Now I planned to slip quietly and blissfully into semi-retirement and jockey my semi over the highways for the briefest amount of time. This semi-retirement arrangement, coupled with a nearly full disability package from the Navy, would assure my continued ability to eat three meals a day. I could afford this.

"Hey Ma, how about Christmas here on the mountain?" She was hooked.

2
Casa Del Fifth Wheel

During the months of divorce wrangling I sought refuge in a fifth wheel trailer parked at the trailer drop-yard of the trucking company for which I'd been attached to more than eighteen years ago. The owner, my good friend Nick, understood my predicament probably better then anyone else in my life. He generously offered the fifth-wheel to me for $500.00. I affectionately named this little haven-on-wheels "Casa Del Fifth Wheel." This minuscule abode was approximately eight feet wide and thirty feet long, the plumbing was in deplorable condition and the refrigerator was permeated with the odor of something that had died months ago. But it was home and stress-free. I bought new bedding, scrubbed the fridge, hung some pictures and welcomed my new-found peace and solitude. However, it soon became very apparent this tiny abode could only serve as a temporary home. A more permanent living solution needed to be arrived at, and soon. And that prompted my trek up the side of the mountain with the realtor lady.

My forested find would shove Casa Del Fifth Wheel into retirement. However she would ultimately play a major role in the evolution of comfort, design and convenience at my mountaintop retreat.

What to do first? My initial plan was to move into the cabin in the Spring (it was late October now) and to live there completely off the grid, independent of all financial demands for services, never paying homage to local utility conglomerates. I figured during the long winter months I would have plenty of time to ready it for civilized occupancy. It currently had no running water, no sewer, no electricity, and I wanted to complete the roughed-in addition before moving in, making it my kitchen. In my work-a-day trucker world I committed to just making the Canadian runs, generating just income enough to fund the cabin's renovations, pay the bills, and feed me. I basked in the glow of semi-retirement at its best. I loved it!

With my focus now totally affixed on the needs of the cabin every day presented new finds: a lumberyard that offered a discount to veterans, a Habitat for Humanity resale shop in nearby Coeur d'Alene, offering a treasure trove of all things needed to transform my cabin from illogically rustic to reasonably comfortable. I discovered a plethora of pawn shops tendering everything I could possible need, plus a whole lot of things I hadn't even realized I *might* need.

At one such resale shop, for a miserly $35.00, I purchased a gorgeous arched window to hang at the north-facing front of my new kitchen artfully framing the mountains and valleys beyond. Once installed, with a table and chair sitting beneath it, I could sup my morning cup of coffee while gazing out upon the mountains and valleys beyond—like a king on a gilded throne surveying his kingdom.

Back in the day radio shows were 'hot' and during the late forties and early fifties The Phil Harris and Alice Faye Show was all the rage. On this show an actor named Elliott Lewis assumed the role of Frankie Remley, a hard-living, trouble making left-handed guitar player. His character served only one purpose: to get Phil into trouble. The trouble usually began when Frankie, in response to a request, complaint or musing from Phil, would speak the line that was to become his signature: "I know a guy . . ." You'll soon realize that I use this line frequently throughout this book, but only because I really do know a lot of guys who readily jump in and help me pull this whole mountain-thing together. Hopefully, unlike the Frankie character, its use will not foretell of troubles in the offing.

I know a guy with a warehouse full of every imaginable trinket, machine, appliance and contraption that has even been manufactured. He invited me to have a look-see. While working my way through his vast collection for things utilitarian, I spied an old Maytag wringer washer tucked away at the back of his shop, bearing a price tag of just $50. It looked to be of the same vintage my mother once used to wash my diapers all those many years ago. I reasoned that once I got electricity into the cabin this bulbous gem would be a godsend, and no more laundromats for me. Thus another acquisition was accomplished. It appeared to be in great shape needing a slight repair—one of its rubber hoses, required to empty the wash water, had rotted out. I was confident a replacement part could be found. Sure enough the internet can find anything. A merchant on the far side of the continent dealt in vintage Maytag parts. Who'd a thought! I have since seen these very same machines advertised for sale with prices ranging from $350.00 to $500.00. Guess I really did find me a laundering gemstone.

Many, many blow-downs litter my ten acres, and the acreage beyond, the harvest of which spelled FIREWOOD to me. In one of the first pawn shops I visited I found just the chainsaw needed to do the job—and priced affordably at $250. I snapped her up, filled her up with good ethanol gas, lugged her to the top of the mountain, and fired her up. She did her job initially—cutting up nearly a half cord of firewood—then sputtered out. I trucked her down the mountain to a repair shop in St. Maries and a day later I had her back. Again she dutifully cut through another half-cord of blow-downs, and again she sputtered out, and again she went back to the repair shop. We repeated that dance two more times. Well, *I know a guy*, a trucking buddy of mine, and this guy knows these machines backwards and forwards, worked with them when they were first on the market. "Ethanol! You're using ethanol gas? You idiot! That's eating all the rubber in the carburetor and messing up the fuel lines. I'll fix this 'ole gal up but from here on in use only premium gas in this baby."

This was just the first of many blunders, missteps and false starts I was to stumble over and muddle through during those beginning days, weeks and months.

Henry David Thoreau believed that people should simplify their lives, and this was in the 1800s. So I wonder what he would say about our world today?

Millions of Americans get up every morning, and sit in traffic for hours, to arrive late at a stressful job, that affords them the funds to pay for the new car (that they will trade up every two years), and the money to pay down a hefty mortgage for a home that is way too big, and used only for their family to eat and sleep in. Why? In pursuit of the American Dream.

I was once one of them. I wanted more; the bigger house, the nicer car, all the "toys" that my friends owned, or lusted to own. The pursuit began to generate bad headaches, and acid reflux. My health was failing fast and coupled with the current list of diagnosed maladies I was on a fast track to an early grave. Sadly, and ominously I have been witness to the deaths of many of my trucker buddies while still in the prime of their lives, and they—in far better health than I.

Don't get me wrong, I feel there is fundamentally nothing wrong with wanting nice things, but the excessive nature of the hunt, the overkill, and the weight of the debilitating debt that trails behind the chase is reeking havoc upon the American Dream. The pursuit of the Dream has evolved into a self-destructive and soul-eroding quest for those of my generation—and the ones following behind. I too would love a spankin' brand new pickup truck with all the bells and whistles. My old gal is twenty years old but with staunch and dogmatic loyalty she still keeps on doing my bidding. Though not the prettiest babe on the road, and a two-time consumer of overhauled motors, she valiantly has kept my vehicle debt at an absolute zero.

We have become the worlds biggest consumer of *everything*. We *must* have every new and shiny gadget that comes along, whether we need it, whether we can afford it, whether or not it even fits our lifestyle. The ad men have convinced us it is so, and adding insult to injury all the gadgets have planned obsolescence built into each and every one of them. Do our computers last more than two, maybe three years? Our cell phones, likewise? Do we care? Seemingly we don't, for we casually toss the old, purchase the next and lust for an inkling into the minds of the manufacturer's next brainchild as it takes shape on his drawing table.

This is the harried world I left behind, and I have not suffered because of it. Would Thoreau be proud of me? Probably not. He'd have wanted me to shed my old faithful pickup and hike the two miles up to my mountain lair. Maybe someday, Henry.

"Life isn't about finding yourself; it's about creating yourself. So live the life you imagined," Thoreau said.

I guess you might conclude that Thoreau's reference to "quiet desperation" might best describe my life prior to acquiring my mountaintop haven. My home life had become such that I was spending as much time as possible away from it and on the road. My 'home' was my truck, my companion, my little King Charles Cavalier Spaniel "Kiyo" and my social life consisted primarily of fellow truckers, conversations in truck stops, and Facebook blurbs with old military buddies from my Navy days. "Quiet desperation" did indeed describe my existence and I hadn't even been aware of it, until the treachery and deceit became apparent. My ultimate divorce can be best described as an escape from an abusive, lonely, and empty existence. I'd forgotten that families laughed together, ribbed each other, hugged and loved each other until I visited my mom and sister in Florida. That was the final eye-opener.

 My mom had grown up in Massachusetts, not far from Concord's famed Walden Pond. Years later, living in Keene, New Hampshire, she had frequently dined at Henry David's, an upscale restaurant built upon the site of the old Thoreau family farm. I had studied the guy during my high school days with feigned interest. His stint at the Pond meant little to me . . . until now. My mom, 1500 miles away, saw the connection, and through the magic of Amazon I had his book in my hands in short order. Now I delved into it with renewed vigor. Dang! I *am* walking in his footsteps! He started with only a spit of land and spent a total of $28 for used material to build his cabin on it. My 'spit' of land—a bit larger—already had a cabin on it but needed the essentials to make it habitable for a twenty-first-century man: fuel, electricity, water and somewhere to put the sewage—aka 'poop'. He lived purposely and alone and shunned his neighbors. I'll be alone most of the time, often isolated by the quirks of weather, but unlike Henry David, I'd met a couple of my new neighbors, homesteading along nearby logging trails, and I rather liked them. Not only that, but they had been most helpful in offering water, advice and a place to park my truck at the mountain's base when the road would, in all likeliness, became snow-clogged, requiring a long trek to my up to my home. But, like H.D., I'd be jerry-rigging most of my comfort accommodations out of used and discarded material and making do without those that I couldn't invent—those niceties that civilized man had come to accept as his god-given right.

3

Meeting Some of My Closer Neighbors

I wanted to close-in and complete the addition the previous owner had begun, add a window to gaze out upon the valley below, knock a door through into the main cabin, and create myself a functional kitchen. The Coeur d'Alene Hospice for Humanity Resale Shop was teeming with building materials crying out to be re-purposed. I perused an eclectic assortment of stove offerings, odd lots of lumber, vast varieties of windows, doors and plumbing options. Ideas began tumbling over each other in my head, and I came away with enough stock to close in and insulate the kitchen, and best of all, to install that beautiful arched window. It would be the perfect addition to the kitchen's valley-facing north wall. I was really anxious to fulfill that dream I held of sitting at a table, with morning coffee in hand, and gazing out through this glorious window to the scene beyond. What a way to start a day!

What a Way to Start a Day!

I spent the next week or so framing in the kitchen and installing the roof. It was slow work for I was dealing with battery operated power tools that kept losing their charge. After numerous trips down the mountain and back to Casa Del Fifth Wheel for recharging I decided it would be prudent to invest in some gutsier batteries and equipment. Work progressed a bit faster then.

I was beginning to get a sense of the local kids on the block. Day after day upon my arrival I spied Moose tracks leading right up to the cabin's front door. And these were no ordinary moose tracks. They were enormous! The Bullwinkle version of sasquatch! And daily the neighboring chipmunks and squirrels piercingly and angrily chewed me out. They objected to the racket, and me just being there in general. Mice had also invaded the place and I just knew we were destined to go head to head over ownership and habitation. But of greater concern to me were the wolves in the area. I had an eerie encounter one night on a trip down the mountain. I had a bit of car trouble, stopped, and while checking under the hood a sudden chill ran up my spine. I looked up to see three pairs of eyes glowing yellow in the headlights. I scrambled back into the car and hightailed it back to civilization. My little pal, Kiyo would be an hors d'oeuvre for those guys, and so I began the habit of carrying my gun with me at all times, and never letting Kiyo wander beyond my reach.

> "A man thinking or working is always alone, let him be where he will."
> —Henry David Thoreau

Pounding Nails Is Very Therapeutic

My future kitchen was all mapped out, courtesy of the former owner. Two-by-fours supported the fledging roof and outlined the floor. I had gathered, found, begged, borrowed and purchased enough lumber to enclose it, complete the roof, lay the floor and hang the insulation. I was anxious to install that beautiful arched window and, once accomplished, I felt my signature upon this place. The squirrels and chippies chattered their annoyance as I pounded in nail after nail. Henry David had nothing on me. He had built his cabin from materials garnered from a neighbor's old barn. Much of my stuff was also derived from other men's projects, reclaimed, reused, and repurposed. It gave me a peaceful kind of gratification I hadn't expected. I was creating something from what had once been a piece of another man's creation. His dreams now flowed through my hands, strengthening my resolve, adding character to my cabin with each board I nailed on. My rhythmic *"nail, bang, nail, bang,—hush you squirrels—nail, bang, nail, bang,— chippies Shut Up!—nail bang, nail, bang, ouch—damn!"* somehow soothed my soul and a healing balm resonated deep inside me.

Chippies Checking Me Out.

I was spending most of my days now up on the mountain and returning each night to Casa Del Fifth Wheel. With my first attempt to spend the night on the mountain I detected a serious lack of insulation between the inner and outer walls. So it became an absolute necessity to carefully remove all the interior finished boards, insulate behind them then re-nail each one back into place. I got a bit artsy while doing it and framed out a rudimentary gun rack and a space for a bookcase. I even created a rough hewn kitchen hutch and devised a few shelves for food-stuff. Before bedtime I fired up the little pedestal iron stove—the only means of heat in the cabin—and I rolled myself into a sleeping bag to settle in for the night. Holy Smokes! I mean really *Holy Smokes!* The cabin filled up with smoke thick enough to burn my eyes. Clearly there was a problem. I toughed it out through the night and come morning I diagnosed the problem. It appeared the stove pipe leading out through the roof was a total misfit and wholly inadequate. I remembered seeing stove accessories and stove pipes in one of the junk shops in town. A quick trip down the mountain with tape measure in hand, a quick purchase, and that problem was resolved before the day was out.

Call it "Shabby Chic."

There Are Vehicles. Then There Are VEHICLES

I'd been babying my 1990 Chevy quarter-ton 4-wheel drive pick up for the past ten years, hoping she would outlast me. Well, she's doing even better than I had hoped for. She's not only pulling her own weight up and down that mountain almost daily, but lugging everything I can stuff into her backside. Washers, lumber, tools and equipment, and even snaking heavy logs out of the woods. I'm right proud of this little red and white workhorse. I regularly pat her on her mottled old head, treat her to sips of oil, lavish her with good gas, listen to her complaints, all the while encouraging her to keep her nose to the grindstone and her tires firmly planted upon the hillside.

While hard at work with the renovation and the ongoing insulation project I still made the time to check out all the available trash and treasure troves. At one such place I'd found not only the solar panels I'd been contemplating but also got the lowdown on just how to install them and set up the battery system. This was a good buy. It gave me a feeling of stability and permanence. With this assembly in place, and up and running, I could power lights, refrigeration, a microwave, my Maytag and perhaps even a TV and Wi-Fi connections. Heck, I could live like a King. Then I found out the bank of batteries feeding off the solar panels could not be kept inside but must be housed in a separate enclosed and dry environment. *Hummm?*

Well, luckily *I know a guy* who wants to get rid of a truck body. It's big, cumbersome, and not very handsome but would provide a dry enclosed environment. It roughly measures 8 1/2 feet wide and 16 feet long and could serve not only as a home for the batteries but a storage shed as well. This guy owns a car-hauler capable of toting that three-ton beauty up this rocky ridge. I figured that once it's set in place behind the cabin I could frame it over, side it with the same rough pine that covers the cabin, and have a proper-looking outbuilding—maybe even doubling as a guest house. Damn! The possibilities are endless!

Future Guest House?

4

About Truckers and Life in General

> "I tend to think of myself and other drivers as mountain men, rather than cowboys. Mountain men lived solitary lives, cowboys were in groups working on ranches. Mountain men roamed free...most called themselves free trappers. Yes, this is what I think."
> —Benjamin Milton Scribner

Here with Son Luke in 1995.

During the years I spent on the road hauling freight from one end of the country to the other—and frequently into Canada, I met a lot of people. All kinds. I've made a lot of friends along the way. All kinds. Many men, some women, many vagrants, some wealthy, many straight, some gay, many generous, some miserly, moral men and immoral men, and every soul along the way added to the tapestry of who I am today. This piece of cloth I bring with me to the mountain.

I believe in the philosophy of what "goes around...comes around." So did Thoreau. I've seen it demonstrated time and time again. It gives you reason to cast out into the universe only the best you have to offer, and chances are you'll find a diamond just around the next corner. (Well, maybe not a *real* diamond, but some facsimile.) The following just might prove my point.

Truck stops represent an oasis for truckers as well as the general population of travelers. Showers are available for truck jockeys to rid themselves of road grime, all manner of vehicles can be gassed up and serviced, there is usually a gift shop filled with trinkets to bring back to those waiting at home, and the food is usually top notch. However, there can also be a flip side to these places. "Lot Lizards" abound. These are the gals, that for a few hard earned bucks, will brighten the night of a lonely trucker and assuage his baser instincts. Best to stay away from these girls. I've seen many a trucker lose a wife and family as a cost of such a dalliance in the bunks of their semis. Then there are those hangers-on who prey on travelers and truckers alike at these sites. They'll have a story—usually a good one—fashioned to make your heart ache, and before you know it their hand is reaching into your pocket. After years on the road, the veteran trucker can spot these guys a mile away. But once in a while you come across a state of affairs that presents you with a truly needy situation.

After a few years on the road, you begin to know who is trying to scam you and who is genuinely in need. I met one such young couple at an Arkansas rest area many years ago. The young man approached me, hat in hand, so to speak, and asked if I could spare a few dollars so he could get some gas for the U-haul truck he had rented to move his family to the next state where a job waited for him. He could not have been any older than twenty, and his wife looked even younger. To make matters worse, they had a baby girl, not quite over the age of one.

I asked him how long he had been on the road and he replied "two days." He had run into a string of bad luck and asked if I could *please* spare him a few dollars for gas and maybe a meal for him and his family. I did better than that. I asked him if he had enough fuel to make it to the next town, where I knew there was a truck stop. He said he thought so. I told him to follow me. I kept an eye on his moving van in my rear view mirror as we pulled back onto the highway. A few miles down the road we pulled into the truck stop and while there I invited them to sit down with me for a hot meal. I think it may have been a stretch for them to trust me as no one else had offered them anything but a hard time. I encouraged them to order anything they wanted and while we talked throughout our dinner they told me about their past. Apparently his former job had ended and there was no other jobs nearby that he qualified for. They had a child to raise so he had scrambled and found another job. Unfortunately it was two states away. When their van broke down it took everything they had to get it fixed. I remember those days well. Never enough money to do anything. Living from one paycheck to the next. Hoping for a better life. Years of hard work just to make it to the next pay envelope. Once we finished our meal they asked if I would watch their baby girl for a few minutes while they attempted to call a family member to ask for additional help. I was a bit taken aback by this request. Most parents would not dream of leaving a young child with a stranger. I was flattered by their trust in me. I played with the little girl while they made their phone calls (No cell phones back then) and had her giggling and laughing by the time they returned. We talked for a while longer about their anticipated new beginnings in a new state, away from friends and family. I could tell they were nervous about this move. They were leaving behind everything that was comfortable and safe. As I watched them drive away I wondered if they would make it. To this day I often think about them and wonder if they are living their dream in their new home. I hope they are doing well, and their baby daughter has grown up to be a young person her parents can be proud of.

    Now as I said, I believe "What goes around, comes around" and the following account is but a small example.

    I have always traveled with a dog, usually a small breed. Just days after rescuing the family from their plight, I was heading south toward Sacramento with my little canine companion Jessie beside me when I spied a check station set up in a rest area by the DOT (Department of Transportation). As I pulled in, and began rolling down my driver's side window I wondered what on earth they were looking for. It was apparent that the officer standing at the entrance wanted to talk with me. The window 'roll down' thing had always been Jessie's cue to the great outdoors and she bounded onto my lap. Just as the officer stepped up onto my running board Jessie and he came face to face, or nose to nose.

"Whoa!" the officer exclaimed almost falling off the running board. "Nice dog. Your co-driver?"

"Yeah" I said. "He does all the night driving."

The officer looked Jessie right in the eyes and said, "Let me see your log book." A log book is a precise record of a driver's daily hours and miles driven as required by the Department of Transportation.

Then he stepped off the running board laughing hard, waved me on through with a hardy "Have a good day!"

I'll never know what they were checking for, but I think my easy discharge and his jovial adieu may have been my payback for helping that family in distress.

I have since considered starting a log book for my traveling companions, and using their paw prints as signatures, just in case I was to run into something like that again.

As stated earlier, "What goes around, comes around." This concept stands me in good stead now and will—well into my future.

"People may hate you for being different and not living by society's standards, but deep down, they wish they had the courage to do the same."
—Author Unknown

The Propelling Force

For years I had been suffering headaches and during the long, intense months of divorce wrangling, they had grown more intense. I'd wake up every morning with a hum-duzzie perched just behind my eyes, eagerly awaiting for me to sit up so it could take over my entire life. My doctor, as concerned as I, ordered an MRI of my head. It showed nothing. That is to say—it did reveal a brain—but no tumors or other apparent causes for the headaches. With my whole being now focused on that little piece of utopia on the mountainside, the angst of the divorce coupled with a dull residual anger at having lost everything I'd worked for these last eighteen years, began to slide away into oblivion. I began to recognize that once settled into my pickup and beginning the now almost daily fifty-mile trek from Casa De Fifth Wheel to the cabin, a noticeable lessening of tension in my back, between my shoulder blades, and the base of my neck. It seemed to dissipate by significant degrees with each mile of roadway I traversed on my climb up to the clouds. And then, miracles of miracles, my headaches ceased altogether! One morning I realized the evil attendant was no longer lurking just behind my eyeballs.

October and the Decision Made

> "Most men appear never to have considered what a house is, and are actually needlessly poor all their lives because they think that they must have such a one as their neighbors have."
> —Henry David Thoreau

"What are you! Crazy!?"

"You can't possibly think you can live on that mountaintop by yourself."

"Oh you'll change your mind come the first snow fall."

"How're you gonna get up and down that mountain when the snow's six-feet deep?" So sayeth all my many friends. They doubted my sanity, questioned my judgment, underestimated my resolve, and seriously misjudged my ability to adapt, wield a hammer, and invent ingenious solutions.

On the other hand, I suspected that just below the surface lay a burning desire to follow in my footsteps. What man wouldn't love a man-cave, far from the maddening crowd, away from all womenfolk, *and* at the top of a mountain?

These rants had been generated on the heels of me expressing the notion that I might just want to move into the cabin sooner than originally planned, like—now.? Casa del Fifth Wheel had become too accessible, with my insufferable former tormentors cruising and stalking, even knocking on the door to offer some sort of perverse olive branch. It scared the hell out of me. My lawyer cautioned I could only seek a restraining order if *true* stalking practices were observed, and could be *absolutely* proven. Well, my guess is if they cruise past my cabin, two miles up the side of a mountain on a barely navigable rutted logging trail, I might just have a case.

Meanwhile I had begun posting pictures of my cabin and its amazing views on Facebook, along with an outline of my plans for living there. Suddenly old Navy buddies began coming out of the woodwork and weighing in. "Wow! How do I get a piece of that!" was the universal response. I was quick to let them know that there were many more acres left on this mountaintop and up for grabs. Only time will tell if they have the "right stuff" to jump on it. Henry David is an acquired taste.

5
Home at Last

Around the end of October I had enough of living in that trailer drop yard and I knew if I stayed there much longer it was not going to end well. The evil nemesis in the guise of my former step-daughter continued to show up at random times with various perverted agendas in an attempt to keep me on their lease. I had to become inaccessible.

My decision made, I loaded up everything I owned that wasn't nailed down from that little wheeled habitat, and hauled it up the mountainside. It took a couple of days and several trips in my pickup but once the bulk of my stuff was loaded, and I took one last visual sweep of the forlorn little refuge, a 'light bulb' went off in my head. Holy Cow! I'm not done with this baby yet! It's heart, liver, lungs and arteries can live on in a new incarnation. The stove, the shower, sinks, the furnishings, even the insulation hidden behind it's tinsel-thin walls can be transplanted into the cabin. Well, *I know a guy.*

Moving Del Casa

That is *I know a guy* who *knows a guy* that has the truck big enough and powerful enough to move Casa del Fifth Wheel up the mountain and to my cabin site. This guy works weird hours and was only available for a move on Sunday the 3rd of November. We set that date in stone.

As luck, (or in this case, probable bad luck) would have it, the evil ex-step-daughter showed up at my door the day before our planned move, all smiles and feigned delight with some cockamamie reason for being there. I cut her short—just being in such close proximity gave me chills—and informed her that as of tomorrow this trailer would be gone, and me with it. Startled, she demanded to know where I was going and my reply was simply that the trailer was being torn down, and that was all she needed to know.

When the next morning arrived I was a little anxious that the "girls" would roam through the industrial park, watching and waiting to see when, and to where, I moved then try to follow. Fortunately, they didn't show.

Nick, boss, owner and friend asked that I also take my old 65 Chevy with me as he needed to clear the yard before snow fell to make for easier plowing. So the same guy that hauled the truck body for me earlier showed up with his trailer. We hooked up the Casa, I loaded up the old 65, then convoy-style we headed south.

By this hour it was raining in Coeur d'Alene—and 50 miles away, on my mountain, it was snowing. Six inches had fallen by the time we arrived at the base. As we prepared for the trek up the mountainside, the *guy* hauling Casa del Fifth Wheel took one look at the situation and uttered, "Damn. I sure hope we can make it."

We gave it a go and about halfway up, with me leading the parade in my Chevy pickup, I was horrified to witness, in my rear-view mirror, the truck towing 'Casa' slipping backwards down the snowy mountain trail. And, he was on a hard up-hill corner with no way to get his wheels straightened out before he and my old home would likely plunge over the edge and down the mountainside.

Miraculously, he was able to stop the slide, straighten out and start the climb back up again. Then, at the next turn the whole thing tried to jack-knife *again*, this time slipping backwards towards the opposite side of the mountain. Now he was *really* stuck!

There was no turning around, or going forward, and not one of us had the foresight to bring tire chains. Stupid? Yes! Damn! Now what?

I walked back to his rig and volunteered to hike back down to the base and into town to buy us some tire chains. I was not looking forward to a long cold trek down the mountainside, but grudgingly I began putting one foot in front of the other in a southerly direction. Somewhere around one hundred feet down the road I heard something coming up toward me that sounded like a real pissed off snowmobile. All of a sudden, like the Calvary to the rescue, here comes one of my new mountain neighbors rounding the corner in my old '65 Chevy, foot to the floor, and motor sounding like it was about to fly apart. Here I must interject. That old '65 was *not* a four-wheel-drive vehicle.

I quickly redirected him to head back down the mountain, into town, to buy all the tire chains he could find. This cost me big time—tire chains aren't cheap. (This was my first meeting with Ernest T. who, with his wife Sherylee, were to become super neighbors and assets to my mountain venture.) Once back with the needed chains, and wrapped tightly around our wheels, we headed back up the mountain. But again we only got a short distance before the weight of the 'Casa' brought us to a halt. So I pulled the chains off my truck, and we wrapped them on the front tires of the truck pulling 'Casa'. Now, with all four wheels chained up, we started making headway.

I told the *guy* (I was riding with him now having left my truck behind) that there was a short way and a long way to get to the cabin. The short way involved at least an 11% grade, and a hard right turn, almost a switchback. The long way was up and around the mountaintop. He chose the long way, good man, *not bad for a former Marine*. (This high praise from a Navy Man). Still, even this route nearly proved to be the undoing of this motorcade. On the way down around an S turn 'Casa' wanted to keep going straight. We straightened her out and finally, the cabin came into sight. I started breathing again, as did everyone else. We pulled in, parked and unhitched. No plan as to the parking location. Just get this thing put, and let's get on with it.

After it was unhooked *the guy* drove me back down to my truck and helped me rewrap my chains. We said our goodbyes, and I headed back up to the cabin. This trip, on a normal day, under normal circumstances takes about an hour. We had begun this venture at 11 am that morning and it was now five pm. I have never been happier to see a day end.

Moving Del Casa.

"What lies behind us and what lies ahead of us are tiny matters compared to what lives within us."
—Ralph Waldo Emerson, 1803–1882

Ralph Waldo Emerson, American poet, essayist, and philosopher was born in Boston, Massachusetts. Known for challenging traditional thought, he became known in literary circles as "The Sage of Concord." Chief spokesman for Transcendentalism, the American philosophic and literary movement, his beliefs and his idealism were strong influences on the work of his protégé Henry David Thoreau, his contemporary Walt Whitman, as well as many other writers of his time. His writings are considered major documents of 19th-century American literature, religion and thought. His philosophies are a strong influent on the doctrines of the Unitarian Universality Church.

Oh my God! Am I mad! Here I am on the top of a mountain, 4,800 feet above sea level, facing winter's wrath, with a stove whose idiosyncrasies I don't yet comprehend, no water, no electricity, and the nearest neighbor homesteads one-quarter mile away. What was I thinking?

Well it's time to put aside what lies behind me, look forward to what lies ahead of me, and discover what lies within me.

On the plus side my headaches have fled and my friends tell me they haven't seen me so happy since they can't remember when. I *am* happy. But I'm also a tad anxious. It's time to assuage my anxieties by making lists. This is a neat way to shift the angst from my head to the legal pad.

On the Plus Side:

I'm on the mountain.

On the *'I Gotta Get It Together Right Now'* Side:

Need more (lots more) fire wood.
Need to figure out this stove.

Need to find a second-hand snowmobile.
Need to find a sled to drag behind the snowmobile to haul up essentials.
Need solar panels.
Need batteries for solar system.
Need to figure out how to install them and tie them all together and make them work.
Gotta find a source for water.
Gotta figure out basic toilet accommodations (probably a composting toilet will do the job and provide me with great fertilizer come Spring).
Gotta find/make arrangements to park truck and/or alternately a snowmobile at base of mountain when roads can't be traversed.

On The *'Need To Solve It Next Spring'* Side:

Gotta get a well drilled.
Gotta look into a heftier 4-wheel drive truck (with plow.)
Gotta take down the small addition on the south side and replace it with a another larger one to function as my bedroom/office with adjoining bathroom and sleeping loft above.
Gotta fabricate a varmint-proof garden.

"If the day and the night are such that you greet them with joy, and life emits a fragrance like flowers and sweet-scented herbs.
That is your success."
—Henry David Thoreau

6

November

"Rise free from care before the dawn, and seek adventures."
—Henry David Thoreau

I wake up in the mornings with Kiyo tucked tightly against me, warm and content under the covers. He greets me with a wet nose and an exuberant lick. I greet him with, "It's gonna be another *great* day."

Oh mornings—and the anticipation of the glorious day lying in wait for us brings me immense pleasure and unbridled exuberance!

I lit a candle last night. I initially did it for light's sake only. However that amazing tiny flicker transfixed my world. It replenished my spirit. This was no ordinary candle. This candle hastened the melting of the day into night, the sweeping of the sun's leftover glow up, over, and beyond the western peaks, and away from my vision. As this candle called forth the night a soothing balm crept into to my tattered heart. It's glow transformed my simple cabin into a magnificent temple, summoning forth all manner of saints and sinners, and all the untold magic of those mystical creatures that dwell in these mountains. This candle, seemingly near-holy, magnified the calm of this night, and the beauty that lay about me. As Kiyo snuggled deeper into my lap, from my perch in the open doorway I gazed out into the night and with amazement, recognized the glow of the lights from Coeur d'Alene, fifty miles away. In absolute silence we two abided in the stillness. Nary a branch creaked nor a twig snapped. Even the wolves and coyotes were still as though mesmerized by day's going and night's coming. And as the nighttime laid down it's cooling blanket over my lofty abode the fragrances of this new world of mine invaded my senses. The absolute silence, the sensual glow of the candlelight, the pungent aromas of the cedars, the pines, and the red firs penetrated my soul, intoxicating me.

I must remember this night. I can't let it slip away once I'm clever enough to bring forth power and light into this raw and pristine world.

> "This whole earth in which we inhabit is but a point is space."
> —Henry David Thoreau

I think I finally have this damn wood stove figured out. Even though it's not the ideal "air tight" stove that I truly need here, I've found that if I stoke it up with hard wood before I go to bed, build up a good bed of coals at the bottom, open up the damper and the vents, and let it run for a few minutes before I shut everything down and go to bed, it will keep me warm throughout the night. Also using red fir (a real good hard wood) at night helps. It burns hot, and when everything is shut tight it burns long, so many mornings I still have coals glowing with enough latent life to begat a new fire without too much difficulty. I've discovered that most people burn red fir or tamarack up here on the mountain. Those trees seem to be the closest thing we have here in the northwest to hardwood. Right now I burn anything I can get my hands on—for this year anyway. Next year I hope to have a rocket stove built (more about that later). I think the rocket stove has the potential to save me money on wood and it's claimed to burn 75 to 90% less wood than a traditional wood stove. I will be doing more research on this type of stove as time goes on. What I've learned: cedar burns hot but too quick; pine smells great but creates dangerous creosote; red fir and tamarack are best for long burning, and on cold, damp days the smell of the wood fire and the smoke that bellows from it permeates my being with an oddly comforting and strangely satisfying primeval feeling.

I need more firewood.

> "I went to the woods because I wished to live deliberately, to front only the essential facts of life, and see if I could not learn what it had to teach, and not, when I cam to die, discover that I had not lived."
> —Henry David Thoreau

Good Neighbors Make Good Graders—And Lots of Other Great Things.

My closest neighbors live just down the road a bit. Actually about a quarter-mile down the mountainside and around a hair-pin turn. I pass their driveway on my trips to and from my 'estate.' They are a young couple with a nineteen-year old son from her first marriage, and two children from this union. Ernest T drives a truck for a local company so it's imperative that he can get up and down the mountain daily. Sherylee is a stay-at-home mom—home-schooling their five-year-old son, and twelve-year-old daughter. Splendid arrangement, that home-schooling idea.

"School failed me, and I failed the school. It bored me. The teachers behaved like Feldwebel (sergeants). I wanted to learn what I wanted to know, but they wanted me to learn for the exam. What I hated most was the competitive system there, especially sports. Because of this, I wasn't worth anything, and several times they suggested I leave. This was a Catholic School in Munich. I felt that my thirst for knowledge was being strangled by my teachers; grades were their only measurement. How can a teacher understand youth with such a system? From the age of twelve I began to suspect authority and distrust teachers."

—Albert Einstein

I tend to be in accord with that Einstein guy.

Ernest T and Sherylee moved here from Montana and this will be there first winter on the mountain. However, having a full year here has prepared them fairly well for the months that lie ahead—unlike me. Ernest T came a-callin' soon after I landed here, offering help and advice. Both were appreciated and both used. I'm the last guy on this road into the clouds, and it's comforting to know both that *I am the last guy on this road* , and also that good neighbors are just near enough, and friendly enough, to be counted on in any emergency. Ernest T's got some interesting ideas for keeping the road open and traversable and is more than willing to extend his plan all the way up to my driveway.

Probably the most important gift they laid upon me since coming up this hill was their offer of water. They had a well drilled when they first moved here, and are willing to let me draw all the water I need until Spring, when I can get my own well drilled. With enough plastic gallon jugs to tote the stuff in, I can drink, cook, and even take a rudimentary bath. (More about that bath later)

And it was Ernest T who brought Larry and Moe into my life, and meeting them was probably the greatest perk and most important asset of my life on the mountain.

I Meet Larry and Moe

> "There will always be a reason why you meet people. Either you need them to change your life or you're the one that will change theirs."
> —Author unknown

Larry's a big guy, over six feet tall, originally from California, however he looks like he could be at home in the north woods of Maine as well as the northern wilds of Idaho. He's the kind of guy that will give you the shirt off his back. He is also the self appointed sheriff of the mountain.

If the mountain had a formal caretaker it would be Larry. He and his wife Moe live at the base of 'my' mountain and he takes it upon himself to periodically navigate all the traversable logging roads just to make sure everything is as it should be. So it was only a matter of time before he and Ernest T came knocking on my door to say "Howdy!" He and his wife have become the most remarkable friends and neighbors a man could ask for. Larry has freely loaned me his tools, as well as his time. He's helped me find blow-downs and other sources of firewood. He's the guy *that knows a guy* in this neighborhood. It was he that discovered through a friend of his that an old man, thirteen miles out of town, was having his property logged. That meant there would be tops and butts left over. (When logging, the loggers have to cut trees to specific lengths for the mills, so they trim the butt ends and cut off the tops that are too small and usually just burned them in a large pile). But Larry heard through the grapevine that the loggers would be more than happy to let us take them off their hands for mere $30 per pick-up load. In general a pick-up load holds roughly one-half cord, and such loads can sell for somewhere between $140 to $200. The cord is the amount of wood that, when the pieces are so arranged and aligned parallel, occupies a volume equivalent to that of a well stacked woodpile four feet high, eight feet long, and four feet deep. Needless to say, I jumped on it. Larry, and I spent a handful of days haulin' choppin' and stackin'. What a boon!

Now Larry's wife Moe is one hell-of-a cook, and generous with the output. She bakes all the time, especially now, as we near the holidays. Many a day Larry has delivered muffins and banana bread to me, fresh and still warm from Moe's oven. Additionally she's a combination nurse, mother, angel, and all-round 'good guy' when you need her. She successfully performed minor surgery on a small wound I had on one of my fingers, and she also has allowed me the use of her washer and dryer until my Maytag gets its new hose, and is operational.

Larry also has a workshop that he's offered to let me use whenever I have project that I can't do, either for lack of tools, or just for a warm place to work.

They have become steadfast and valued friends in the short time I have known them.

7

It Still Tends to Be All About the Firewood

My chainsaw died again today, and as I need to cut more wood this is a big problem. Lesson learned: never buy a chainsaw from a pawn shop. I borrowed one from Larry, but it's small and not up to the task, so at Larry's suggestion we drove down into town to the local 'saw-shop' to see if they had any good used ones on hand. As luck would have it they had quite a few. All of them had been thoroughly gone over and serviced. I picked out a likely candidate. The shop owner started it up for me and vowed it was capable of meeting all my needs. So for $250, plus the cost of a spare chain, I bought it. I really didn't want to buy another saw right now, but I've been cautioned that I'll need another eight-cords of fire wood if I am going to last the winter out. So the purchase ultimately became a no-brainer. I was also told that my old saw will cost more than it's worth to fix, but I think I'll hang on to it and fix it anyway. It would be nice to have a spare around—just in case. I really think it doesn't need that much tinkering to make it right. I might even dive into it myself during the long cabin-bound winter months. Besides, *I know a guy* who can get me the parts I need, and what the hell, I used to tear down torpedoes in the navy, so how hard can a chainsaw be?

I still need a bunch more cords of firewood.

> "Every man looks upon his wood pile with a sort of affection."
> —Henry David Thoreau

My Domain Gets a Name

It was serendipitous. I was returning from a trip into town with my head full of things that needed to be done, all the while spouting off about my new digs to a friend via cell phone. "I'm heading back up to Chez Walden," I said. "Bingo! Chez Walden! That's the perfect name for my sweet abode!" Unfortunately my friend doesn't know squat about Henry David Thoreau, or Walden Pond, or even what a 'chez' is and was sure I'd just gone off my rocker. But the name felt perfect. *He knew—Henry David*—and I'd like to believe at that moment he reached across the century, through the cosmos, and placed his seal of approval upon my wilderness venture.

Kiyo is getting used to the more stationary life on the mountaintop, so much so that I worry about him. He's become complacent and has developed the habit of wandering off while I'm working outside—not good, as wolfs prowl nearby. We are in their range, squatting in their territory. I've also been told of a mountain lion up here. Haven't seen his tracks yet, but do see a lot of moose and deer tracks around the cabin. They don't seem to be coming quite as close to the cabin as when I first invaded their territory, but by their tracks they let me know they are close by. My Mom reminded me of an enterprising soul who some years ago made a decent living refurbishing moose droppings. Yeah. That's right. *Moose poop*! This marketing guru created rather elegant Christmas corsages from moose droppings—after having laminated them first—and marketed them as "Moostleltoe." My Mom sold several gross of them in her gift shop back in the seventies. As I recall she also carried fancy drop earrings (no pun intended) made of the same stuff. Maybe there's a cottage industry here just waiting for me to exploit it.

It seems to me that throughout my years on this earth moose have randomly moved in and out of my life. When I was just a lad of about four or five, I looked out the window of our home in North Wakefield, one of the sweetest little villages in all New Hampshire, and spied a huge moose on our front lawn. He had green antlers. I ran to tell my parents about this awesome discovery only to be met with a disbelieving and disinterested response. Apparently I was prone to tall tales at that age so my report didn't even garner a flicker of interest. However, later that morning my Dad found huge moose tracks in our driveway, leading across our lawn, crossing over the road, and heading into the old sandpit across the way. I was exonerated. The "green" antlers were another matter. Then a seasoned wildlife friend told my parents that when moose shed their antlers each year, the residue that dangles haphazardly from their bony outcrops looks moldy-ish, possibly *green* to a little boy.

Years later, as a teenager my family lived in the shadow of Moose Mountain in Brookfield, New Hampshire, probably the second sweetest town in the state. Moose Mountain boasted a small ski resort and its facilities were free to all the kids that resided in Brookfield. Each winter my sister and I, plus all the neighborhood kids, spent most of our waking non-school hours on those slopes skiing, snowmobiling, and rollicking in its frigid embrace. It was a heck of a way to grow up!

Then there was that other moose. The Rocking Moose! This magnificent piece of art was crafted by a master woodworker and designed for children to ride on. His head rises above my waist and the breadth of his antlers measures over three feet. *Think of Bullwinkle with rockers.* My Mom sold the works of this craftsman in one of her gifts shops and when my youngest son was of an age to sit upon it, she gifted it to him. My wife hated it. It spent most of the next decade in storage and away from her sight. Fortunately for me, because of this aversion, it came back to me in the divorce settlement. Bullwinkle now resides in my cabin, commanding a front row vantage from the edge of the loft, where he can see and be seen supervising all comings and goings.

Now here I am, deep in the heart of moose country, surrounded by them, being curiously observed and scrutinized by them, and enjoying the hell out of it.

> "The moose will perhaps one day become extinct; but how naturally then, when it exists only as a fossil relic, and unseen as that, may the poet or sculptor invent a fabulous animal with similar branching and leafy horns, — a sort of fungus or lichen in bone, — to be the inhabitant of such a forest as this!"
> —Henry David Thoreau

Last night Kiyo got himself all folded up in the hide-a-bed I salvaged from Casa de Fifth Wheel which temporally doubles as my bed. I was having a problem unfolding the dang thing so rather than continue to fight with it I folded it back up, returning it to its couch-like state. Once done I went to the kitchen to look for a snack, came back, and sprawled out upon it. After a few seconds I realized Kiyo was nowhere in sight. I began calling him. He didn't respond. Unusual. Somehow that normally smart little pooch had crawled under the contraption and while I was folding it back up and got himself trapped beneath it. He never said a 'word'. Not a bark, not a whine, not a whimper—nothing at all! But boy was he a happy pup to be out from under it. I bet he won't do that again.

Kiyo

I need more firewood.

Do you see a reoccurring theme here? It's called *anxiety*.

I spend hours searching out blow-downs scattered throughout my ten acres and beyond. I haul them back to the cabin and between bracing cups of coffee saw them into manageable pieces, then chop them into firewood. As I watch the wood pile grow I feel somewhat reassured regarding my supply of life-sustaining heat. But I still need more. I'm told it will take over eight cords of firewood to see me through the winter. It looks to me to be about two cord now.

"Chop your own wood and it will warm you twice."
—Henry Ford

Having researched a little about solar energy I've now determined my previous solar power plans are inadequate to handle my needs.

I will need bigger batteries, and more of them, as well as far more solar panels. As of now my stock consists of just three solar panels, producing 45 watts—on a good day. This allows me light for two small lamps. I believe I will need at least twelve of these panels, however, twenty-four would give me a total of 500 watts. I think that number plus a small wind turbine should provide enough energy to fulfill the needs of this small cabin. Also, I plan to cannibalize my old 65 Chevy pickup for its alternator and fan to construct a homemade wind turbine. I think I might even be able to utilize its gas tank. I can mount it on a sled—the one I plan to build and drag behind my snowmobile, when I get a snowmobile—and haul it into town for fill-ups to fuel my backup generator—the one I just bought from the same guy that sold me the Maytag washer. It's an old generator—ravished from a dead motor home—and my plan is to install it in the old truck body and hook it up to the cabin for an additional 110 volts of power. This may help keep the batteries charged as well.

That's my plan.

The Beginning of My Solar Energy.

My desperate need for a means of keeping warm throughout the impending months of winter remind me of a yarn my father used to relate about an old guy he once knew. Dad and his brother Bill were just kids when they first met Rufus. Now, to fully get the gist of this story you must appreciate that Rufus was one of the last of a dying breed of old Yankees— one of those men who lived frugally and sparsely. He resided on a few hardscrabble acres near my grandfather's farm. My Dad and Uncle Bill would frequently visit old Rufus as much for the tales he told, as for the blackstrap molasses he would smear on slabs of bread and offer to the boys. He had his own way—pretty ingenious really—to keep warm in winter. Come the first frost, he would herd all his cows into the cellar beneath his ramshackle dwelling, and move all his chickens up into the attic. The animal heat from the cellar radiated upward, warming his house, while the years of accumulated layers of chicken manure deposited upon the attic floor above trapped the warmth and provided excellent insulation. Pretty low-tech but it worked. Clever as it may seem, cows and chicken on my mountain would never work. But it's interesting to contemplate.

I need more firewood.

I have begun hooking into my pickup truck's battery at night, allowing me the luxury of watching movies on my TV. Without this 'truck-perk' the TV would draw so much power it would quickly kill my current arrangement of solar-powered batteries. I know at best this is but a short-term solution because very soon I doubt that I will be able to drive the pickup up here.

8
Well. I Knew It Was Coming

Canada. I had agreed to take all the loads going into Canada and Nick, my trucking boss and friend, wrestled one up for me. *Gee Nick, you really didn't have to do that. I've still got a lot of firewood to cut and stack.*

My plea didn't so much as scratch the consciousness of Nick and so with great reluctance I gathered up my trucker's gear, whistled to Kiyo, and off we went. Back on the road, sitting over 18 wheels and behind 500 horses, I was, in a way kind of relishing this break. I'd been steeped in planning, constructing, devising and agonizing over my pending winter survival. This would clear my head. I'd always loved the trucker's life, being on the road, seeing this vast and beautiful country of ours. I loved chatting with other truckers in truck-stops. I've always been lucky in meeting and making new friends, and trucking gave me the opportunity to meet up with these road-bums again and again as we crisscrossed America. I heard the most fantastic and wonderful stories from some of them. From others I heard of their pain. As mentioned earlier, they have, unknowingly, contributed to the weave of my life's tapestry.

I remember one old guy, sitting alone in a booth in a northeast truck stop. He seemed to be pondering his life over a steaming-hot cup of coffee. He was dressed all in red flannel, smoked a Meerschaum pipe, and his face was wreathed in a fluffy white beard. Good Lord! If he didn't look like Santa Claus! I slipped into the seat across from him and for the next hour or so we share a congenial lunch and some good conversation.

He lingered on my mind for the next couple of days and a story about him slowly began to evolve in my head. Now, I'm not a writer, but my mother is. I shared my ideas with her and she begged to flesh it out. Well of course I said "Yes!" And of course she did. And that story won the Mark Twain Award for children's literature the following year. She titled it "Ben's Christmas Gift". It was about an old trucker-guy with a beard, a 1934 firecracker-red Mack truck, his Missus, his reindeer, the little guys who tended them, and well—you know—he's jolly old St. Nick. Wonder what that old guy in the truck-stop would think if he knew he'd been immortalized in a children's story.

So here I am on the road again. Wonder if I'll meet anyone interesting on this trip?

The Canadian run—up and back—took about five days. It was not so much fun. These pesky maladies I'm suffering with are aggravated by the pounding of wheels to pavement. I couldn't wait to get back to my mountain. Then too, the headaches returned with a vengeance. Trucking for me was just not fun anymore. I'll be happy to keep it at a bare minimum.

Finally I began the climb back up to my Chez Walden retreat, and with each turn of the wheel the ache in my head drained away like sand sifting through an hourglass. Home.

I'd been looking for a snowmobile—one that I could afford. It turned out Nick's stepson had a snowmobile for sale. It needed work—not sure how much yet—but the price is right at just $600. It's an old three-cylinder Polaris and it should be gutsy enough to climb the mountain. I hauled it to a repair shop and a week later was informed that all it needed three new pistons. Other than that it's a good machine. I told the shop to go ahead and service it, replace all the fluids and belts while they had it. Now I have the machine to pull the dogsled I'm planning to rig together.

I have begin gutting Casa del Fifth Wheel. Both the kitchen sink, and the propane range have been pulled out and more-or-less installed in the cabin. I say more or less because the sink is only a temporary installation, and the stove's gas line and tank are still inside the house, as I'm lacking a special fitting to hook it up outside, plus a box must be built to house the propane tanks. Will finish this up soon.

I've also pulled out most of the drain pipe from Casa for later use in the cabin. In time, I plan to yank out all the wiring for my planned 12-volt light system. I hope to have everything cleaned out of her before the snow collapses the ole' dear. She's served me well. Her harvested organs assures her continuing life.

Most houses powered by solar and wind power run on at least three "banks" of batteries, each totaling 48-volts, which then run through an inverter to produce the 110-volts required to run a household. Since I plan to run my cabin on 12-volts, with the exception of the fridge and the washer, all I should need are a few more and bigger batteries. I wonder who came up with the 110-volt standard? Since 12-volt lights work just as well as their 110-volt counterparts, this seems strange to me. There are many 12-volt appliances that work just as well as those requiring 110-volts. This I know as a trucker. Many 12-volt appliances are sold in truck stops. They perhaps run a little bit slower but they still do an adequate job.

Casa Del Fifth Wheel.

Lesson learned. Don't stack your firewood adjacent to your cabin wall. Of course it would seem the logical thing to do. For ease of access it makes perfect sense. However one must take into consideration what a devious snowstorm can accomplish. With the advent of the first six-inches of the cold white stuff, it gathered briefly on the roof, picked up a little weight, then stealthily cascaded down and over my fledgling woodpile, nearly blanketing it completely. My first job the morning after the storm was to exhume the pile, move it, restack it piece by piece in location less convenient but further from the cabin's steeply inclined roof.

I'm losing weight. Between the wood-chopping, the renovations, the trips up and down the mountain, and the fact that while keeping so darn busy preparing my cabin for winter survival that I simply forget to eat. Apparently my stomach isn't too concerned about it, for it never complains, rumbles, nor begs to be coddled. I've shrunk two belt-notches. Who knows? I just might become so fit and svelte up here at Chez Walden that I'll become a hot 'chick-magnet'. That'll be a first.

"People love chopping wood. In this activity one immediately sees results."
—Albert Einstein

In 1995, the U.S. Fish and Wildlife Service introduced 35 Canadian grey wolves into central Idaho and the Yellowstone area of Wyoming as an experimental introduction. This, because the Idaho Timberwolf population in those areas numbered less than eighty. These wolves quickly multiplied and now roam in large packs of 20 or more in the rural areas of Idaho, western Montana and western Wyoming. These aren't your run-of-the-mill wolves. They are a very large breed of Canadian grey wolf that can weigh upwards of 180 lbs. They are huge, dangerous and "kill for fun," preying on moose, deer, livestock, pets and even small children. They are quickly depleting the native wildlife population thus impacting the state's lucrative sport of hunting.

I heard wolves last night chasing something down in the woods behind my cabin. It was around 11 PM and I had come awake to stoke the fire. While loading the stove, the wolves began their strange chorus of barks and eerie howling as they chased some poor creature down. I just hoped it wasn't the cow moose or her calves that I'd recently observed in the neighborhood. That would be a real tragedy. These wolves brought down from Canada, are not native and not a good fit for this area. They have been killing off the elk herd and the moose herd, as well as depleting the deer population. Out of state hunters no longer come here to hunt for there is nothing left for them to hunt. These wolves are killing off the sport.

This morning I started in early chopping and stacking firewood and while doing so I put Kiyo in the truck for safe-keeping. Though he could still see me, he wasn't a happy puppy; he likes being near me. I explained to him that it's far better being closed in the truck cab than getting eaten by a wolf or a coyote. On the heels of my warning I heard a coyote howl, and it was close by. I think that may have convinced Kiyo that perhaps "Daddy Knew Best." I made sure my pistol was cocked and ready should that become necessary but I guess he saw me first and went the other way. In this part of the world coyotes are considered vermin. There is a bounty on their heads. I don't believe in killing animals unnecessarily, and would do so only in extreme conditions—if I, or my dog, was threatened.

Not all critters on this mountain are cause for alarm. I took a break to go inside to warm up and get some coffee, then headed back outside to my woodpile. To my amazement, a large flock of chickadees had gathered in the trees surrounding my cabin. Chickadees, here! Never saw them here in Idaho. But they looked like chickadees, they sounded like chickadees, so they must be chickadees. They appeared to be looking for food. I told them to come back again in a couple of days and I'd have some for them. Have to make a note of that on my grocery list.

"I once had a sparrow alight upon my shoulder for a moment, while I was hoeing in a village garden, and I felt that I was more distinguished by that circumstance that I should have been by any epaulet I could have worn."
—Henry David Thoreau

9

My Escape Clause

"What is human warfare but just this; an effort to make the laws of God and nature take sides with one party."
—Henry David Thoreau

Ali Al Salem Air Base in Kuwait is a Kuwait air force installation with part designated for operations by the US Air Force and its allies. Ali Al Salem Air Base is a small, yet highly guarded base in Kuwait. There are no permanently assigned US aircraft, with only USAF and Navy transient aircraft and a squadron of British Tornado fighter aircraft. "The Rock" provides combat rescue, theater airlift, aero-medical evacuation, air surveillance and control, theater ballistic missile defense, as well as force protection, combat support and the ability to survive and operate for coalition air, ground and other operations. The Landstuhl Regional Medical Center (LRMC) is an overseas military hospital operated by the United States Army and the Department of Defense.

Me. Guarding the Waters of the Persian Gulf.

I've talked a bit about the tapestry of my life and those souls I've met along the way who have contributed to its weave. A huge piece of my cloth was woven by my Navy buddies and tempered during the year I spent in Kuwait. The months spent there provided me with a whole new prospective and generated a short-fuse when having to deal with petty and whiny people. Their issues sour in the face of the trauma and pain I've been witness to.

I have seen the face of war. No—not actual combat—but its horrifying aftermath. My unit was charged with guarding the only deep water port in the Persian Gulf and our orders were to protect our ships as they unloaded their vital war supplies for our troops "up north." We were not directly privy to the goings-on in the hell north of us. We simply facilitated the fuel that fed that madness.

Christmas Day 2005: As I took a seat aboard a medivac flight bound for Landstuhl Regional Medical Center in Germany I inwardly cringed, feeling like a deserter and a fraud. I felt I had abandoned my friends, my buddies—the guys I had bunked with, chowed down with, worked side by side with, shared stories and dreams with, and all because I'd been broadsided by, until now, a seemingly insignificant little gland in my neck. And here I sat on a plane, surrounded by men and women—many of who were the ages of my kids—with mangled bodies, wounds and traumas of such great proportions that I guessed many would never fully recover. Here I sat among them on this flight only because my thyroid had betrayed me. (That was my initial diagnosis- there was more to come) Then, shortly after we took off from Ali Al Salem Airbase in Kuwait, we landed again in a forward base "up north" slightly akin to the fighting-zone. What happened next profoundly affected my life—both then and now. As a forty-four-year-old, I'd been considered the "old man" of my squadron, and the poor bastard that was being carried on board at this stopover couldn't have been more than twenty, and maybe weighing a buck twenty. He was wheeled onboard on a stretcher, and dragging behind him was about three hundred pounds of medical equipment—there just to keep him alive. The entire plane went quiet. None of us on board had the courage to look at him. He had been a turrent gunner on a Humvee, and had the 'luck' to have been thrown clear when an IED (Improvised Explosive Devise) blew up right under it. Yes, he had survived, but in an extended coma, oblivious to the fact that none of his pals and comrades had survived.

It is a humbling and overwhelming experience for a middle-age man to be witness to the devastation perpetrated on fellow warriors a generation younger than himself. Here was I, brought down by a silly gland and sharing vital medivac space with this poor bastard, barely out of his teens, who would probably not live to see the States again, his home, his sweetheart, or his mom.

Then, once at the hospital, I mingled amongst the wounded, some with jaws wired together with screws and pins, and some with arms and legs, or half a face missing. I experienced the horror of an attempted suicide by the young sergeant occupying the bed next to mine. So many injuries. So much mental devastation. So many ruined lives—so much pain and cruelty inflicted upon America's finest, our kids, our young fathers, our most beloved. We send healthy and whole young men off to war, and broken old men return.

I think about this daily; that kid wheeled aboard the medivac plane, the suicidal young sergeant, the ruination of American's best. I wondered then if the folks back home had *any* idea—did they *really* know what war—*this* war or *any* war—is all about? And the shattered progeny it spawns? Maybe they think they know. They may have first-hand knowledge of their former paperboy who went off to war and came back without his legs. But do they *really* know? How could they? The media can not possibly convey the true horrors, the multitude of devastated American youth. It's not just their neighbor's kid or the few local soldiers they read about in their daily newspapers, it's thousands upon thousands. *And why?*

To this day, I can't think about that plane ride, and the men and women I met while in that hospital, without tearing up. And I think about them often.

"War is an ugly beast, a nasty thing, and no one comes away unscathed.
The closer you were the deeper the scars."
  —Benjamin Milton Scribner

Then I Came Home

Nothing looked right, felt right, nor sounded right anymore. I attempted to resume my former life, but my former life no longer existed. I had been profoundly touched by my experiences in the Gulf and no one here seemed to give a damn. Everyone around me carried on with their petty lives, cursing out the driver in front of them for going so slow, complaining about the late mail arrival, wondering what dress to wear to the next party. Bullshit! It was all bullshit! Don't they know what's happening over there? Can't they as least pretend to care? Millions of American lives had been changed—my life had changed—and nobody gave rat's ass.

I quickly grew weary watching old friends and acquaintances go about their daily lives as thought it was their God-given *right* to be the first in a line, their *right* to be selfish and demanding, their *right* to behave in an arrogant manner if they didn't get their own way, their *right* to conduct their lives in meaningless, small-minded pettiness. Their supercilious attitudes meant *nothing* to me anymore. Good Lord. Had I once been like them? I simply no longer had tolerance for it. And sadly, it was happening in my own home, in my own marriage. I discovered, purely by accident, that my wife, under the perverse guidance of her devious daughter, had begun divorce proceeding while I was still stationed in Kuwait. Under the same preposterous influence, it was quickly shelved when it was determined I was deemed 70% disabled, and would be receiving a generous monthly disability check. Oh ain't love grand?

There has not been a day in my life since I watched that poor bastard being carried on that plane that I haven't thought about him, wondering if he lived or died—and if he lived—was it a life worth living? His memory will forever be a painful token of that war, one that returns to haunt me again and again—as an unwelcome guest during my waking hours—as an evil genie of my midnight dreams. And forever, that kid, that victim of "collateral damage," will unbidden, cause a catch in my throat, and bring tears to my eyes.

This is one of the reasons I ran away. To escape the crap. To seek refuge on my beautiful mountaintop.

"War is Hell"
—William Tecumseh Sherman

10

The Lovely Ancient Agatha Comes Into My Life

I was heading back to Chez Walden from Coeur d'Alene with my pickup truck overflowing with more stuff destined for my cabin comfort. As I was about to make the turn onto the highway heading south, I spied a old iron cook stove in the window of a corner pawn shop. Can't resist a find like that, so of course I pulled in to have a look at it. At first glance it appeared to be in pretty bad shape, though the main body was still intact. She had a few missing and broken parts but I guessed they shouldn't be too hard to find via the internet, (Though ultimately my internet search for the Maytag hose prove futile. Wrong part sent.) I asked the price, and while we haggled back and forth over the listed price, I spotted a rustic homemade dog sled nearly hidden in a corner of the shop. Ah-hah! It would exactly fit-the-bill to tow behind my soon-to-be-purchased snowmobile for hauling much needed supplies and materials up the mountain road when it becomes impassable by truck. I had planned to build one—but here is one—already built and ready to go. I offered to pay the $200. asking price if he would throw in the sled as well. He agreed! I was thrilled. I got both pieces for the price of the just the stove. I told him I would be back for both on the following Saturday. I was pretty excited about these finds. The cook stove, once restored, will make a great addition to my cabin. Not only will it provide additional heat, but it also has a water tank on one side, which will take care of another one of my needs. The name *Ancient Agatha* popped into my head as I continued my trek up the mountain. *Where the heck did that come from?* Then I remembered an article my Mom had written and published in *New Hampshire Profiles* years ago about *her* old black kitchen range. As a long-standing family joke she had christened her warm-breasted beauty after an old flame of my grandfather's. So—*Ancient Agatha* she will be. And Grampa, your legacy lives on. *Please look down on me from time to time.*

Ancient Agatha.

With Agatha coming on board, my kitchen floor plans will have to change a bit. I must rearrange the locations of where I had planned to place the sink and gas range—courtesy of Casa del Fifth Wheel. The placement of the rustic hutch I built will have to shift as well. I'm anxious to search the internet for replacement parts for her and begin restoring her back to her former gorgeous self. The oven door, in bold iron relief, boasts her birth name—Floral Banquet T model 620-G. She's an old girl and in much need of a lot of TLC. I believe there is a company in Massachusetts that specializes in parts for these antiquated gems. I'll have to do a bit of research. It will be a good winter project.

I Knew It Was Inevitable.

It was inevitable. It's going to get cold. The night finally arrived when the temperature dropped like a bomb, and with astonishing suddenness the thermometer registered below 0. Then the wind picked up. It must have been howling around the cabin at 20-miles-per-hour. It ferreted out and invaded every nook and cranny, every feeble flaw in the cabin's construction. It was painfully evident that my futile attempt at adding insulation here and there as I detected a pressing need was woefully wanting. The previous builder never properly closed in the area under the eaves, between the rafters and the top of the supporting outer walls, (the soffit), thereby leaving openings big enough to throw a cat through. Insulation alone would not solve that problem. I will have to rebuild the entire underside of the roof overhang. Furthermore there should have been OSB plywood installed first, before any of the siding went on. Without it the wind just trucks right on through. It was also painfully evident that more insulation was needed in the ceiling, where the stovepipe exited. Oriented strand board (OSB) is an engineered wood panel product made of resin-bonded wood strands or flakes. The wood strands are precisely cut and oriented in order to produce a wood panel with uniform strength and density. Like plywood, it is widely suitable for use as a structural board, and is commonly used in roof and wall sheathing, in subfloors, and increasingly in furniture manufacturing.

Since that first cold night I've been patching every hole I can find, but the bigger issue can't be addressed until I put on the new addition next summer. In the meanwhile I'll throw more wood on the fire, heap on more blankets, and cuddle up closer to Kiyo. When Spring comes I plan to tear off the existing roof, insulate as it should have been done initially, and install new—all green—metal roofing. Currently there seems to be just metal roofing resting on rafters. Not good.

Ahhhh. A Bath At Last!

I had been searching for a bathtub that would mesh with, and perhaps even enhance the cabin's rustic ambiance. Something old, antique-ish, perhaps an old claw foot tub. Then I stumbled across a brand new livestock watering trough for just $130. It's six feet long, two feet wide, two feet tall and I think it will do the trick. On her side blazes her name in big red letters: TARTER. With a hole drilled in her bottom, and PVC piping attached to drain water to the outside, it should fit the bill for the new bathroom I plan to build in the Spring. Then I will plumb in a shower head to hang above, and rig up something to heat the bottom. The tub's bottom that is—not mine. This should be easily accomplished by simply installing heat tape under the trough, the kind folks up North affix to their roofs to prevent ice buildup. In the meantime, it can serve me as a portable bathtub.

My Spankin' New Bathtub.

The Silence of the Lands

Imagine a pristine world. No sounds, no honking horns, no crying babies, no screeching brakes, no motors running, no household noises, or telephones, or TVs, or radios. That's my world. My forest is mostly silent. Occasionally a chipmunk scolds, a wolf howls, a moose may step on a branch, but the sounds from the booming little city of St. Maries lying below in the valley never reach through the clouds to puncture my piece of paradise. The only hint of the civilized world beyond is the infrequent drone of a airplane passing overhead as it makes its decent into St. Maries' small airport. This stillness, this silence, enters my being, soothing me, touching on the sacred. This alone is worth the price of Chez Walden and all its future needs, demands, and upgrades.

"I never found a companion that was so companionable as solitude."
—Henry David Thoreau

Well the time had come to test the validity of my new livestock tank. Even Kiyo let me know that my infrequent trips into town for a quick shower at the local truck stop was just not doin' it. I put a sixteen-quart pot of water on the stove to heat and dragged the TARTER inside. Dang! She takes up more room than I thought she would. But if I'd settled for the smaller four-footer I simply wouldn't have been able to stretch out full length in it. Once the pot of water grew hot enough I set it into the tub, climbed in buck-naked, and straddled it. Damn, the bottom was cold, yes, both mine and the tub's! Next time I'll figure out a way to warm the bottom before getting in (the tank's not mine—though it will certainly benefit mine!). After the initial shock, with chilblains traveling all the way from my arse up to the back of my neck, I grabbed an old broken handled coffee mug and began pouring the warm water all over myself, from head to toe. Then a quick soaping, a quicker rinse, and done. Immediately upon crawling out—wet and sans towel—I dragged the tank to the door, up-ended it and dumped its contents on the ground outside. Holy Cow! The below zero-temperature stung like a thousand hornets! I need to get that drain installed and plumbed in pronto. Bottom line: Kiyo was grateful for my efforts and willingly cuddled up close to me at bedtime.

    Next day a light bulb went off in my head when I realized sometime ago I had purchased a camp shower for possible use in my truck. It was probably still buried deep in Casa del Fifth Wheel. Then I recalled the heating element no longer worked, however I believed the pump still did. I went in search of it and sure enough, there it was hiding under some debris in the old Casa. I dug it out, put in fresh batteries, pushed the button, and what do you know, it still worked. This will make future bathing a whole lot easier. No more dipping a coffee mug to wet, wash, and rinse. I will still have to drag the tub outside to drain it, but that will be taken care of soon. I'll get that hole drilled, attach a drain, then plumb it to the outside. It'll stay in the back room for now, though it's damn cold back there. But I can solve that problem too. A small propane heater was left behind by the previous owner and it runs on those small propane bottles that I can buy at any Walmart.

11

Ernest T Rocks the Road

"Friends... they cherish one another's hopes.
They are kind to one another's dreams."
   —Henry David Thoreau

Ernest T builds a plow...or is it a wannabe road grader?

My "next-door" neighbor, Ernest T had heard of an ingenious road grader and plow the loggers of the area had devised and successfully operated for years. They were made from large logs and dragged behind their trucks. These clever devises were used to grade off, as well as plow, the rough-hewn roads gouged from the forest's floor, enabling their trucks an ease of access in and out of the areas being logged. Commonly called back-blades, they had become essential to their operations. A back-blade typically is made from a thick log—usually eight-feet in length or more—split in half lengthwise. The two halves are mitered together at one end to form a V then bolted between the open legs, another split log—of approximately half the length—or four feet long—would be bolted to each leg forming a triangle. The whole thing lays flat on the road with the point of the V facing toward the back of the truck. The unit is then chained to the truck and dragged behind for a very effective road-clearing. Not only would this effectively remove all rocks, roots and other debris, but smooth and grade the road as well. It works just as efficiently clearing snow from a roadway.

Ernest T's back-blade was made from an eight-foot log and dragged behind his pickup would clear about a four-foot section of road.

He proudly showed me his devise and invited me to join him for the inaugural run, his agenda being the need some extra weight on the thing. He asked if I was game. Sure—I'm up for anything that looks like fun and will keep our road clear—and more importantly—participating in any advancement in the name of science. So with me perched precariously on the cross-piece of his dubious but clever contraption we rode down the mountain roadway—then back up again. Woo Wee! What a ride! Aside from the cold—I could see my breath—and the wet snow cascading over the top of the blade—the raucous dips and turns in the road, and the banked corners—it was one hell-of-a ride. *And it worked!* Half way through our Grande Experiment of sweeping clean the mountain corridor he holler back to me, "How ya doin'?"

I bellowed back, "It's a little chilly back here!"

He yelled, "I'll turn up the heat!"

Ernest T's Road Grader.

"If it's both terrifying and amazing then you should definitely pursue it."
—Erada

Now on the heels of the success of this prototype Ernest T plans to build an even larger and heavier one. One designed to clean the whole road the just one swipe.

That first snowfall, on the day we pulled ole Casa del Fifth Wheel up the mountainside was just a teaser, an omen of things to come. The next storm, dumping two-feet of snow over overnight, left no question in my mind as who really was the boss of these Idaho mountains. The morning after that storm I had to dig out everything. All the wood I had hauled in, cut, split, but not yet stacked, was covered under the frozen white stuff and much of it stuck fast to the ground. Stupidly, I had left my splitting maul outside overnight and it now was invisible, hidden somewhere underneath all this mess. It was imperative that I find it. Had to find it. Forgot where I had last laid it down. An hour of digging, turned up my gas can and chainsaw oil—I forgot that I had taken them out of the pickup the night before—but no maul.

That First Big Snow and All My 'Stuff' Rendered Invisible.

This early snowstorm prompted me to get my Maytag moved inside and under cover for it too had begun to freeze to the ground. This baby is my pride and joy and didn't want to chance her getting damaged while sitting outside any longer. I was still in a quandary as to finding the missing hose I needed to make her fully functional. The part I had ordered from an online supplier had proved to be the wrong one. I found a guy in town that has quite a few old Maytags at his place of business. His sweet old aunt had put me in touch with him. She has one from 1948—it was originally her mother's—and it still looks brand-new. She wants to sell it. I was tempted to buy it, but urgency demands other things right now, plus I still believe I can make my own gem useable. So now, *I know a guy* , and he is looking for the part I need, and if he can't find one he believes he can modify a piece to fit what I already have and make it work. I left it in his hands. (If his aunt still hasn't sold hers by Spring I may buy it. I just love these old machines.)

I think I might *finally* have enough wood to last the winter. I hauled in two more loads last weekend. It's still "green" but if I add enough dry wood with it I believe it will burn just fine. Next year, probably around August, I will start ordering my wood for the following winter. I have too much else to do here to be messing around with scouting out blow-downs and dragging them back to the cabin. I would rather pay for the stuff then spend valuable hours traipsing around the mountain scrounging it up. This decision hopefully is a wise one and will free up precious time to work on projects inside the cabin when the weather's not favorable for outside work. And when the weather-gods favor me there'll be free time to move forward with outside projects. Inside projects when the weather's nasty and outside projects when the sky is blue, and the breezes balmy. Yep! That's the plan.

Another lesson learned. I have come to the conclusion the batteries I bought, which I thought would do-the-trick, aren't going to be up to the task of keeping everything running in my little abode. So now I've begun the search for more appropriate ones—and I think I just may have found them. Nick showed me a large forklift battery he had recently purchased, to replace one that had died. It can generate something like 1200 amp hours, and the cost is in the vicinity of $150. I'm considering purchasing four of them to replace those I bought earlier. I've also found better solar panels for sale on craigslist. They're used, but still offer far more output than mine (only 45 amps on a good day). Just one of these used panels will put out about 150 amps, therefore installing three or four of these, to supplement those I already have, should supply enough power for all my electrical needs. I am still attempting to locate a better regulator for my solar power set-up. Also, I have found via the internet, a source that sells wind turbines. I could purchase one for as little as $400. One that would put out 600 amps would totally fill my needs. Then, of course, I would need a tower, and better regulator for sure. So between heftier batteries, more and better solar panels, augmented with a backup generator, I should be kept living in total comfort.

"There Must Have Been Moon Glow"

Recently, on the heels of a brilliant moon-lit night, I thought I detected a storage increase via my four existing solar panels. I did a bit of research on that possibility and found the general consensus is—no—the moon can't or doesn't have what it takes to generate enough energy to store. But I know what I saw. There are some advocates, however, who do believe a slight benefit may indeed be had from a very bright moon. Science is pursuing this possibility—everything from solar panels *on* the moon to finding methods of harnessing it's potential here on earth.

About That AC/DC Thing

It seems that back in the late 1880s Thomas Edison and Nikola Tesla were embroiled in a 'pissin' match,' now known as the "War of the Currents."

Edison developed direct current (DC) which runs continually in a single direction, and it became the standard in the U.S. Problem was: it is not easily converted to higher and/or lower voltages.

Comes along Tesla believing that alternating current (AC), which reverses direction a number of times per second (60 in the US), and can be converted to different voltages via a transformer, was the solution.

Edison, not wishing to lose royalties, began a campaign to discredit the AC theory, even spreading rumors about it's dangers.

Now along comes the 1893 Chicago World's Fair when Edison's bid to electrify this event using DC was out-bid by George Westinghouse using Tesla's AC.

That same year the Niagara Falls Power Company awarded a contract to power it's Falls to Westinghouse—who had licensed Tesla's polyphase AC induction motor patent. Polyphase is a means of distributing alternating-current electrical power.

On November 16, 1896 the entire city of Buffalo was lit up by the AC from Niagara Falls causing General Electric to jump on the AC bandwagon too—seemingly obliterating DC. Fast-forward to today: our electricity is predominantly powered by AC, our computers, LEDs, solar cells and electric vehicles all run on DC power, and new methods are now available for converting DC to higher and lower voltages. Furthermore since DC is more stable, companies are finding ways of using high voltage direct current (HVDC) to transport electricity long distances with less electricity loss.

So it would appear the War of the Currents may not yet be over, but instead of continuing the 'pissin match' between Edison and Tesla, it appears the two currents may end up working parallel to each other in a sort of hybrid armistice.

And none of that would be possible without the genius of those two men.

Edison also said "We don't know a millionth of one percent about anything."

The Blessing of Good In-laws

Many years ago as a youthful sailor I served as a torpedo-man. My job entailed the maintenance those bad boys, and a large part of that job required a pretty firm knowledge of electronics and electricity. Well, a skill not used is soon forgotten, so when I began floundering through the dynamics of wiring my cabin I was a bit at a loss. Lucky for me, not only do *I know a guy* who knows this stuff inside and out, but he's a member of my own family. Enter my brother-in-law Steve. A rocket scientist for real! He's probably the smartest guy I know—well maybe—he married my sister so the jury's still out on that. (You know I'm just kidding Bess—love 'ya.)

Here's his take on it.

"Many different types of batteries and other electrical products are available in the marketplace, but I am going to focus you on just what's needed for a 12 volt system. There are two types of 12 volt batteries: one is a lead acid variety, and the other is a gel type. The former has two shortcomings—it gives off a poison gas when charging and discharging, and another drawback is if it drops below freezing, it will freeze and become utterly useless. The gel has no such shortcomings."

He brought up another issue that I hadn't even considered yet, regarding the quantity of sunlight my solar panels would be exposed to during the long winter months. I told him it would, no doubt, be low. Though I'm almost at the top of the mountain, my property is surrounded by heavy forestation, consequently during the dark winter months the panels may experience a significant lack of sun-exposure. However, I do get a lot of wind up here, so he suggested I rig up several wind turbines to offset this shortcoming. Great idea Steve! Wow—how great it is to have genius at arms-reach.

In the 12 volt system that I'm proposing for my cabin, the batteries must be kept close to where the power will be needed. This because the resistance increases over distance and the shorter the wire run the less voltage drop. Electricity is similar to water in that the voltage behaves much like water under pressure, and current or amps flow in a water-like manner. Resistance goes up when the hose is small and down when large. Amperage is the flow of energy through the wire, therefore, if the wire is too thin for the current needed it will heat up much like the coils in an electric heater, and the energy will be wasted because it's generating heat. If I am to use 10 gauge wire, it should carry all current needed—at 12 volts—for the appliances I will be using. The power that an appliance uses is referred to as watts. Ten gauge wire is used in car cigarettes lighters because they "draw" a lot of watts to heat the lighter element. In fact, a 10 gauge wire at 12 volts can carry 360 watts of energy.

Should I Invest in Band-Aids or Shin Guards?

When splitting oversized hunks of logs into manageable pieces of firewood the separated chunks generally fly apart and land away from the splitter (me), usually ending up somewhere near the growing pile of ready-to-burn firewood. Once in a while however, they will change direction—as if in retaliation—and hit me right in the shins. This hurts. I cuss. And if I notice blood running down my leg, will head to the cabin for a band-aid. My legs are beginning to look like the end result from a war-torn country's mine-field. Moe suggested I wear shin splints. Good idea. Next time I'm in town I will look for a soccer player and ransack his backpack.

My Plan #?

My plan is to finish the kitchen first—from the floor to the ceiling—all the wiring—all the plumbing, and then—when winter moves on—and the weather becomes agreeable—I will deal with some of the larger issues. I will take off the roof, put down OSB plywood, and then new roofing (still metal, but all one color—green). Once I'm assured of the efficiency of the kitchen addition—air-tight—and wind-proof, I'm determined to tackle the bedroom add-on at the rear of the cabin. I recognized almost immediately, once moved in, that it was sloppy construction—perhaps an old chicken-coop, re-purposed and added on as an afterthought. I plan to tear it down and build a larger addition to house an office/library, and bathroom/laundry room at ground level, with a full-size loft above for my bedroom. Once I've completed that project I will go to work on the main cabin, first tearing down the ugly existing loft, to fully expose the vaulted ceiling, then remove the wood paneling on the north and west walls (only the walls on south and the east side will remain wood-paneled, the others will be drywalled). While those walls are open and exposed I will run wires, install a vapor barrier, and fill in any and all places missing insulation—and there are many. By next winter that I should have the whole place tightly wrapped, efficiently roofed, and I can live snug-as-a-bug-in-a-rug.

12

The Big Question

The subject on everyone's mind—but the one nobody dares to ask, (an issue the astronauts and I have in common), is the subtle "toilet-question." This property has no indoor plumbing—no running water—no outhouse—so what do you do? Well—I'll try to be as delicate as possible. Here's the skinny:

I keep a camp toilet in the cabin. It's not very glamorous but highly functional. Come Spring when I add a bathroom addition it will include a composting toilet. The end results (no pun intended) of this toiletry gem will be a boon to my future garden. Meanwhile, back to this winter's solution. When this lot was cleared all the trees that were cut down to make way for the cabin were piled into five substantial mounds about the property. A rather large pile of these ravished tree trunks and rotting limbs is situated near the end of my driveway. I plan to burn this mound when we have more snow on the ground, but for now it makes a good depository for the daily accrual of waste material as well as the ashes from the wood stove. The ashes prove a good covering; eliminating smells and thus discouraging the possibility of unwanted guests. Once this pile of tree residue and waste is burned over it will become a great area for my composting heap. There I will dump anything and everything rot-able where it will ultimately provide me good soil for my future gardening. (I figure if moose-poop and bear-poop are good for the environment, can people-poop be far behind?)

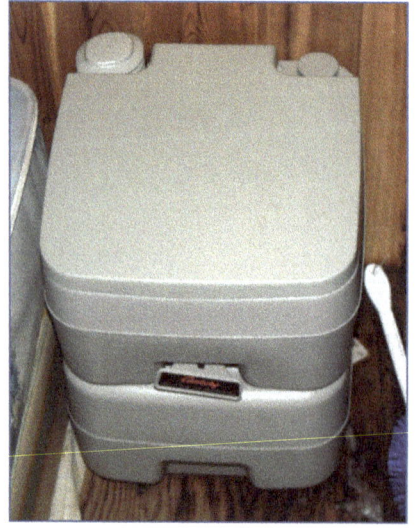

A Typical Composting Toilet.

Dumpster-Diving of the Highest Caliber

Two dumpsters sit at the bottom of my mountain, near the main road, tantalizing the passerby with a plethora of riches. Great pickin's for anyone willing to paw through someone else's castoffs. Now—I have not been dump-picking since I was a lad living in small town New England. There in that rarified utopia it was the god-given right of every townie to check out the dump's latest arrivals on a regular basis. And there, almost always, you could find something of value to *you*, if not to its previous owner. At my newly discovered mountainside cache I have resurrected, and hauled back up to the cabin, a "new" recliner, a whole bunch of pulleys (I can always find a use for these), and a few feet of plastic drain pipe, always needed. Apparently I am not the only passerby to reclaim and recycle other's abandoned treasures from this trove. It appears to be a pretty regular pastime for many of the local residents. Example: I recently deposited an old couch there on my way into town and it had been snatched up before my return trip (As ye sow, so shall ye reap). This has become an habitual stop on each of my trips up and down the mountain, and I have reaped much.

My Dumpster–Diving Treasure.

"There is one consolation in being sick; and that is the possibility that you may recover to a better state than you where ever in before."
—Henry David Thoreau

Woe is Me

It's never any fun to get sick, and it's *really* no fun getting sick in a cabin, on a mountaintop, all alone and with a fire needing continual attention. Just to go for help, or sympathy, or a couple of aspirins at this time of year, requires an able-bodied man to put chains on his tires just to get down off this damn mountain, and then remove them once there. *Sorry, it's the fever talking.* And an ill man is not an able-bodied one. But that was exactly my predicament recently.

It was a Saturday morning when my throat began to feel a little scratchy. I thought that if ignored, it would go away. But by midnight I could not breath unless I was laying on my left side. This is not good I thought. I really didn't want to attempt a trip down the mountain, to scout out the local emergency room facility. The whole chaining and unchaining thing was more than I could handle. Luckily I rallied a bit on Sunday morning and did negotiate the trip down into town to pick up some medicine. After that I don't remember a thing. For two days I lay in bed. I guess I did manage to throw an occasional log or two on the fire, but don't really remember even doing that. I didn't know if it was day or night, a Monday, Tuesday or Wednesday—and didn't care. When I finally began to feel better I pulled on some clothes and negotiated my way down to Larry and Moe's place. The first question out of my mouth was to asked Larry what day it was. He laughed and told me it was Tuesday, then he and Moe invited me in and fed me. I hadn't eaten anything for two days and I must have looked like the wrath-of-god. Moe fixed me a couple of scrambled eggs, toast and set a steaming hot coffee down in front of me. I made quick work of that and then she heated me up one of her amazing homemade burritos. I felt much better with a full stomach and decided I'd probably live. Those two wonderful neighbors have been the best thing that has happened to me since I moved here. I don't know what I would do without them.

Mom Sends a Care-Package

Mom's decided not to spend Christmas up here with me. She's

gonna wait 'til essential plumbing is in place. Claims her out-house days are behind her (again no pun intended). But she's with me in spirit. I've just opened a huge box sent from her via USPS. It contains the most eclectic assortment of stuff imaginable. I'd complained of the mice sharing my abode. So to thwart the little devils and protect my perishables she included a rusty old decorated tin breadbox which had, ironically, belonged to me during my first marriage some thirty-years ago. Why she's kept it all these years is a mystery. Well, not really—she's a Yankee after all—it's in her blood. Inside the breadbox was a WW II ammunition box that once belonged to my Uncle Charles. I had loved him dearly in life and will treasure always having a piece of him on this mountaintop with me. And inside that, sat an antique toy iron milk-truck, which I had purchased the previous year from a second-hand shop in Florida while on a visit to Mom. I begged her to repaint it to make it look just like my Grandfather's 1930's milk truck. And oh my, does it ever! Even his name and phone number—*Francis W. Rose - tel. 121*— appear in miniature on the driver's door.

Grandpa's Old Milk Truck in Miniature.

For ballast and packing she had stuffed in packets of exotic soup mixes—touted as easy to prepare on a stove-top—a can of B & M baked beans and another of B & M brown bread, (in deference to our New England roots and our Saturday night suppers, The Burnham & Morrill Co. of Portland Maine were the suppliers of choice for our baked beans and brown bread), a toy for Kiyo, a swatter for the flies (they relentlessly appear from their hidey-holes every time the cabin warms up), a couple of Christmas ornaments which included a glass pickle—a nod to our German heritage, a stocking filled with an assortment of batteries (always needed), another stuffed with candy (always appreciated). She had also tucked in a box of band-aids in camouflage décor, and a bottle of headache tablets. To keep the contents tight and rattle-free, she stuffed in several rolls of toilet-paper. I felt like a kid on Christmas Eve as I pulled each treasure up from the depth of the shipping container. Each piece stirred a memory. Each piece calculated to brighten and enhance my mountaintop retreat. Thanks Mom!

My Next Plan #?

If I make it through this winter—and I will!—come spring I plan to tear off the existing poorly-built add-on and build a larger, more energy-efficient, addition to include a *real* bathroom with plumbed-in Tartar tub complete with a shower head, lavatory and a composting toilet. My Maytag will also take up residence there. My Mom suggested I hinge a couple of shutters together to form an artsy concealing buffer for the washer. My response? An immediate "Hell no! I want it to show! That's the prettiest dang thing here in this cabin. I gotta show it off!" This addition will attach behind the main cabin on the south side and boast two entrances to the bathroom, one from the kitchen, the other from the office.

Larry is trying to convince me to design my addition as an ell rather than simply adding to the existing dimensions of the cabin, which would give it a shotgun look. I'm turning that idea over in my mind, and I'm starting to like it. It would definitely give me more space in the "upstairs" loft providing for additional storage, plus a larger office below, with lots of space for my book collection. I might just do it.

13

I Wax Poetic

> "This is a delicious evening, when the whole body is one sense, and imbibes delight through every pore."
> —Henry David Thoreau

Nightfall. The most splendid hours on my mountain. I steep in the quiet. I restoreth my soul. I marvel as the windows to my outside world slowly dissolve, evolving into looking glasses—each one a mirror of my inside world. I wonder if I'm the only one who has ever witness this phenomena. One must sit and be still to see it. The little blaze I set earlier chugs away in the belly of my wholly inadequate pedestal stove. She gossips to me of the day's events in a language we both understand—words shaped 'round the snaps and crackles produced as she consumes her evening's fuel allotment. Sitting front and center is her bulbous front door which frames her hot, fire-bright rectangular face beaming through a worn and pitted glass-front. She watches us—Kiyo and me. She is doing her darnedest to provide for our needs—giving us the best she has to offer—radiating heat—conveying a kind of friendliness—an inviting mellowness—all spawned by the blaze I begat in her iron innards hours ago. She companions us—makes us a threesome in these waning hours of daylight—resolute—striving to do the right thing—*to keep us warm.* She's become a dear little friend, a willing comrade, and an alarmingly essential accomplice in our forthcoming battle—that of our survival throughout the impending and harrowing months of winter.

Does she know? Can she possibly sense the fate awaiting her once the ice, cold, snow and bluster have spent their furry and moved on? Can she perceive that come spring she will be dismissed, discharged, discarded, thrown out and traded for a more efficient heating system? Would she continue to befriend us if she knew of her impending demise, once Winter breaths his last? I really hope not. 'til then, dear inadequate little friend, we shall fight this battle of survival together. Both, giving it our best.

"Night is certainly more novel and less profane than day."
—Henry David Thoreau

On A Scale of 1 to 10: How Bad Was Your Day?
(One being a bad hair day. Ten being the end of the world)

"If one advances confidently in the direction of his dreams, and endeavors to live the life which he has imagined, he will meet with success unexpected in common hours."
—Henry David Thoreau

> *Mamma Said There Would Be*
> *Days Like This*
> *There Would Be Days Like This*
> *My Mamma said . . .*

We all have days when nothing seems to go right—when everything that can go wrong—will. Today was one of those days. First off—the damn stove will not stay lit. Then a seven- gallon water jug leaked its entire contents all over Ancient Agatha—froze to it—and then carpeted the floor with a layer of ice. It was a veritable skating rink at that end of the kitchen. As I planned to work in that corner it was necessary to employ my hammer to bust the ice from the floor. Once done and the floor safe for walking I went about the job of installing the gas range, newly harvested from Casa del Fifth Wheel. There were only a limited number of 2x4's to do the job so I couldn't afford to make any mistakes. Well, I did. I cut one piece to the right length, but I cut the other one too short. After much cussin' and kickin' I wrestled up a couple more 2x4's from the scrap pile outside and this time managed to make the proper cuts. Using some of the short pieces I'd messed up I finally got the job done. Then came the hooking up of the gas line. I wasn't able to extract the regulator out of Casa del Fifth Wheel, so used the spare stowed away in the shed aka "Guest House". However,

I did manage to get the copper gas line out of Casa—the one that goes between the stove and the outside wall—or so I thought. I drilled all the necessary holes, ran the gas line, and then to my dismay determined both ends of the line were female. So back to the Casa I go. I found the proper fitting but in my feeble attempt to extract it, stripped it and now it's locked in place. So for now I have the rubber hose attached to the stove and the propane tank is sitting nearby—in the house. Not a good thing. Rubber and fire do not go well together. The whole affair is jerry-riggin' of the lowest caliber. This will have to be watched closely until I can find the right fitting. Once found, the copper line will hook up to the rubber one on the outside. Some sort of devise will have to be rigged for outside storage of the propane tanks to keep them moisture-free and prevent the regulator from freezing. So far this day has been a series of piddley setbacks and frustrations. Winter breeds such challenges, and what can't be avoided or overcome must be endured. Humor aids endurance. I must learn to laugh a lot. Mamma said there would be days like this.

> "I have always been regretting that I was not as wise as the day I was born."
> —Henry David Thoreau

St. Maries

The little town of St. Maries (pronounced St. Marys) is nestled at the foot of my mountain, and my lifeline to all things needed. Settled in a lush valley at the confluence of the St. Joe River and the St. Maries River, it's set among spectacular mountains, rivers, lakes and forests—ostensibly providing an almost theatrical scenic backdrop. Located just a two-and-a-half hour jaunt from the Canadian border, it is the county seat of Benewah County, with a population of about 2,800. With the Rocky Mountain Range traveling from its top to its bottom providing an elevation of 2,192 feet above sea level, it is the bedrock measure of my lofty 4,800 foot mountain retreat.

The local economy is driven by the timber industry complemented by some mining operations and a solid base of farming. The remarkable beauty of the area combined with the exceptional quality of life has spawned a comfy retirement community in the area. The local mill whistle blows every day at 7 a.m. and 3 p.m. and can be heard nearly all through St. Maries. It's a dull, tinny hum that hangs in the air for a full seven seconds. But no one really takes notice—a telltale sign of life in a small town.

The townsite was selected by Joseph Fisher who built the first sawmill in 1889. He had the foresight to recognize the potential of the nearby lakes and rivers to provide for the transporting of logs to the mills, and steamboats to transport finish products to markets. The city was officially established in 1913 and when Benewah County was formed and St. Maries was named its county seat.

It is a thriving community boasting two airfields: St. Maries Municipal Airport and Sky Island Ranch; a high school, middle school, elementary and alternative school; a Baptist, Presbyterian, Lutheran, Seventh Day Adventist and Foursquare Church, and is home to Benewah Community Hospital. It hosts a library, several motels, inns, several Bed & Breakfasts, and borders on the Coeur d'Alene Indian Reservation and Casino. It also provides me with all the my essentials: hardware—dumpster-diving—a bevy of clutter-shops—and groceries.

On Labor Day weekend St. Maries comes alive with her annual Paul Bunyan Days celebration, offering three full days of logging competitions, water events, Moto-cross races, carnival rides, food & craft vendors, music, fireworks and parades.

A great little town to have cozily snuggled at my feet.

14
The Path

> "Eons ago in the fires that forged my soul
> Fate laid down the path I was to follow.
> Many lifetimes have I followed this road—
> Upon the deck under British sail
> Amid the cannon's roar,
> At Gettysburg I faced the Blue in Pickett's fatal charge,
> In a Corsair above the Philippines I held the Japs at bay,
> I have lived and died so many times and still...my path goes on.
> Now once more I find myself upon this cursed way.
> My soul howls...
> Fate laughs...
> And I once more..."
> —Benjamin M Scribner, written during first enlistment, circa 1979

A Friend In Need

> "The most I can do for my friend is simply be his friend."
> —Henry David Thoreau

An old comrade in arms called me today, just as I was getting ready to head back up to Chez Walden. His wife had just suffered a heart attack and had been hospitalized. He was beyond distraught and reaching out to anyone who would share his pain.

It hurts me so to see any one of my old comrades and their families grow older and suffer the infirmities of aging. I was the oldest one in our Kuwait unit. Most of the guys (and gals) were just kids when I first joined the Navy in 1979—some not even born yet. Then when I reenlisted years later I took quite a bit of good natured ribbing from them. I was alternately referred to as the "boson's mate on the ark", or the "a gunner's mate on Old Iron Sides." Now we are all getting older—time is catchin' up with us. Most of my old comrades have since retired from the Navy Reserves and gone on to other things. This particular friend who just called me will be retiring later this year. The old unit is gone—disbanded.

I asked my friend if there was anything I could do to help. He was tired, distressed, in need of sleep, so he didn't even know how to answer that question. But he knows if he needs anything, I will be there. We have stood beside each other many times in the past.

When I reenlisted just after 9/11 no one could believe that I left a job in the trucking industry, where I made pretty darn good money, to go back into the military. Compared to the wages of the guys I was serving with, what I had earned driving a truck seemed a small fortune to them. My reentry back into the Navy garnered me one hell of a pay cut.

But what is money all about anyway? Unencumbered now by the women who leached everything from me, I have all I need, or want, with just enough left over to help a friend in need. Recently, when the home of one of my old shipmates burned down, just before Christmas, I made sure she and her family had what they needed to see them though the holidays.

On more than one occasion I have seen fit to subsidize an old comrade in need. Frequently these men (and woman) will be on orders that can change from month to month and sometimes, when there is a squabble over in Washington, they might not see a check for an extended period. In a perfect world our troops would, and should, be paid more than the tired old men and woman who sit in the halls of Congress and 'run' this country. I don't know what I can do for him for just now but if he asks, I'll be there.

"The character inherent in the American people has done all that has been accomplished; and it would have done somewhat more, if the government had not sometimes got in its way."
—Henry David Thoreau

Back to the Mountain

I had mentioned earlier that I was considering a couple of

interesting options for heating the cabin in the winters to come. One really creative, and apparently extremely efficient, heating system is called a rocket stove. There are many good video's on the internet these days describing these stoves. YouTube has a number of them. The more I watch these videos and learn about them the more I'm intrigued by their design. The theory behind their effectiveness is that once the wood is placed into the small fire box, the heated air is drawn through into a combustion chamber made up from two 5-gallon cans with the ends cut out and welded together. Then a six inch stove pipe is placed down through the center on these cans and a material called 'cob' is slathered on to fill the space between the stovepipe and the five gallon apparatus. All this is then covered over by a fifty-five-gallon drum with one of its ends cut out. (I am oversimplifying this but the details are online for the viewing) The exhaust piping exits from the bottom end of the fifty-five gallon drum and its tubing can be run back and forth through a kind of settee or bench that is totally mudded over with the 'cob' mixture. ('Cob' is a material made up of one part clay, three parts sand and a small amount of straw to bind it all together.) The heat then transfers into the cob which emits a slow and even heat throughout your home. Another big plus;—there is almost no ash left as the burn is 99% complete. Another advantage; should the fire go out, the cob will hold its heat for a long time and continue to transfer warmth into the home. And as if these pluses are not enough to convince me, here's another: these stoves will burn anything that will catch fire, from pinecones to pallets, and one of these stoves will consume 75% to 90% less wood than a conventional wood burning stove. Think of the savings. The more I look into this type of heating system the more I think this might be ideal for my needs. If I run the piping through the wall of my "living room" into the new addition it should heat my whole place, though I might still install a small wood burner in my bedroom for those really cold nights. No sense being cold if I don't have to be, and I'm finding that it gets damn cold up here—and this in a winter that's reported to be a mild one. I'm going to assume that when I get all the mistakes fixed that were perpetrated by the last owner, this place should stay warm and toasty, even on the coldest nights. Now if I can just keep the road open.

15

Ya' Know There—Mr. Winter. You're Beginning to Act Like a Big Bully.

Windy as hell today, and tonight...*very* high winds. I'm hoping that by tomorrow it lets up. I'd planned to help Larry get his roof fixed. He wanted to do it today but Moe didn't want him up on the roof, reattaching the metal roofing, in this wind. Can't say that I blame her. She cooked burgers for us today after the power came back on (the wind had knocked it out for a while), and then we sat around and chatted for a bit while my dirty laundry did a turn in Moe's washer. During a brief lull Larry and I went out to take a look at the roof and while we were out there a wind gust nearly took off part of the roof over the main house. We quickly grabbed some screws and anchored it back in place before the gale could do any more damage. This left me a bit concerned that two-miles up the mountain my roof might be getting the same treatment—but when I got home all was well. It would seem my little cabin is tucked away in just the right spot to be protected by the embracing hills.

There's a small nine-hundred watt generator on sale at a local big box store in town and I'm thinking about buying it. That size should help me keep things livable around here until I can get my *really* big generator up and running. It won't be powerful enough to run the fridge but it will help keep the batteries charged. Now that I can no longer can get my truck up the road the battery-thing can spell a real problem as I was depending on the truck's battery for some of my power. Yeah—the wind and snow created a bit of a road issue and I had to leave my pickup at Ernest T's place. Tomorrow I plan to hike back down to my truck, then back to Larry's to help him fix that section of roof over his shop - that piece of metal roofing was blown off in yesterday's high winds. I also hope to get some end-of-year paperwork done while at Larry's- utilizing his power.

Ernest T's wife Sherylee, is freaking out about getting snowed in up here. I'm concerned that she may not make it through this winter if we're not able to keep the road open, and honestly, it does look a bit dubious. The drag will not work effectively anymore because of the bankings of solid-packed snow and ice that have built up on both sides of the road. Once those snowbanks freeze hard the road will close in becoming narrower and narrower and nothing will get through except perhaps a snowmobile. I'm not worried. Been in tougher spots. It might be a pain in the arse to get in and out of here, but it's my home and I refuse to leave. I do have other places I could go to wait out the winter, but that would spell defeat. Anyway, there's always my snowmobile.

> "What you get by achieving your goals is not as important as what you become by achieving your goals."
> —Henry David Thoreau

Well, we managed to get Larry's roof put back together, though he's going to have to replace most of the metal roofing come Spring. Parts of the metal sections that we'll have to remove are still in pretty good shape—lengths long enough for me to utilize to cover my kitchen roof—with possibly enough left over to cover my proposed addition as well. We'll see. If it works and it's newly painted the whole thing will look brand new.

While at Larry's I spied a bunch of 2x4's thrown in a pile over the bank. I asked what he planned to do with them and he muttered that they were just junk—too full of nails to be good for anything. I looked them over and told him that I didn't mind pulling nails and anyway, I wanted to use reclaimed old lumber. He said, "Take 'em!" There looks to be at least twelve, maybe more. I'll have to dig for them but boy, can I use them. With winter bringing outside work to a screeching halt I'm getting a little bored. Pulling nails will give me something to do and (maybe) enough to 2x4's to frame in the upper ends of the cabin over the big window. I'm planning to frame over the two small windows in the rear as I wouldn't be needing them once I add on this spring. Now I can get those ends insulated and tighten this place up a bit more.

Going into Coeur d'Alene tomorrow to pick up a few things, and will take a second look at that small generator. The price came down again from $99.00 to $89.00 so it seems like a good time to buy it and

I should probably jump on it. Until I can get the big one put in place, and up and running, this smaller one will help make life here more bearable.

It's snowing here again, and will be throughout tomorrow. Then we're promised nice weather for a few days. I'll use that lull to dig out some of my wood that's buried around here and split it up. I'm close to having all my stockpile split and ready to burn. I figure if I split for an hour a day during the next few days of good weather, I just might be done with it. Then once it's all stacked and I can start (maybe) shoveling out my "yard" so as to make it easer to get the snowmobile turned around. It's a heavy one and turning it around by hand is a bitch. Would rather just have a large enough clearing to turn it while it's moving.

Kiyo is not a fan of riding the snowmobile. He takes personal offense at the noise. I thought he'd enjoy it. He loved riding with me on my four-wheeler last fall. Hopefully, by the end of this winter he'll be used to it. The alternative is for him to stay behind at the cabin while I run up and down the mountain to do errands. He'd hate that more than the snowmobile ride.

My cell phone stopped charging last night. It's currently sitting in my truck at the bottom of the mountain at Larry's place. To further compound the communication issue my house phone needs a charge, leaving me without any form of outside contact at all. Kind of scary—another reason to install that nine-hundred watt generator. Among other duties it can carry out will be to keep the house phone operational. I'm slowly inching toward a civilized existence up here, and not sure if that's a good thing or bad. I kind of like things the way they were, but there are people who still need to get in touch with me and I with them.

Sherylee is getting more serious about getting off the mountain for the duration of the winter. She can't handle it up here. Ernest T says he will stay here, but I don't think he will for long—if she really does leave. If they do go, it will leave only me up here with my closest lifeline—Larry—at the bottom of the mountain. That's two-miles down a steep, winding, snow-blocked, and maybe soon to be un-traversable logging trail. This will make my survival up here quite a bit more challenging—the biggest issue being water. I've been getting my water, a gallon at a time, from Ernest T's well. As for traversing our roadway, I think I can make it with the snowmobile as long as the road doesn't ice up. Another possible problem would occur if the snow accumulation gets ahead of me. I'm told that by this time of the year there would usually be five to six feet of snow on the ground. Thus far Ole' Man Winter's been pretty easy on us and only dumped a couple of feet. But he will most likely come roaring in like the bully he's reputed to be during February and March. I'm concerned that my ability to get the snowmobile up this hill could be greatly compromised.

Yesterday I *finally* got the last of my belongings out of Casa del Fifth Wheel. With an accumulation of two feet of snow heaped on her roof and I feared she might collapse. But *I know a guy* who wants her for scrap and is willing to haul her down the mountain when spring arrives—collapsed or not. Fortunately he'll take her even if she's become a pancake. It's amazing how much stuff I had tucked away in her bosom. I'll miss the little darlin'—a little. Everything of importance that I had stored in her is out, but I still hope to salvage some of her waterlines and pipes, plus her 12-volt water pump, and maybe even some of the 12-volt wiring. She was a good ol' gal while she lasted—my refuge—and a willing provider of so many essentials for the cabin. Now it's time for her to put her out to pasture.

16

The last few storms have buried the rest of the wood I still need to split, so now I dig one log out at a time, split it and stack it. This will no doubt become an arduous chore as the snow is deep and crusty. Oh well, nothing better to do here on the mountain while winter and her elements, snow, ice and wind have their way with me. I keep finding wood I didn't know I had, most of it's still green, but by the time I need it, it should be dry enough to burn. Though green wood will burn, it is harder to ignite and takes a hotter fire to keep it going. It also produces more creosote so I have to be careful not to put too much of it in the stove at one time.

Went into Coeur d'Alene yesterday and picked up that little generator I've been hankering for. I have it set up near the cabin's front door and so far it seems to be working out just fine. It's giving the batteries the boost they needed and now I can watch movies on the TV for hours before it needs to be gassed-up again. While in town I also picked up a snow rake to pull the deep snow off my various roofs, as well as the truck body. It does a great job of raking off the snow buildup. I cleared the accumulation off the truck body as it had built up to a depth of almost two-feet. I can't let that cave in on me—it holds everything I own that wouldn't fit in the cabin. I also had to shovel out from in front of its doors so I could get inside. I decided that next year I will own a snow blower. That would make my life up here so much simpler. After accomplishing all those tasks I headed around to the back side of the cabin to rake off the kitchen roof—and sank up to my knees in snow. Not fun. Next time I attempt this I'll strap on my snowshoes.

My Brand New Generator.

Evening is settling in. I've brought in enough wood for the night, and it's getting down-right chilly outside. I say 'chilly' because it's been in the high 30s today so 'til now it's felt relatively warm outdoors. I too am settling in for the night, cooking beans and hotdogs. This is a typical Saturday night supper in New England, but I felt like cooking it tonight, Wednesday. I hope I don't offend any spirits from my New England roots. Even though the fire is chugging along nicely in the stove, warming things up just a enough to make the cabin cozy, I still cover up with a blanket as I sit and read. No sense wasting good wood when a warm blanket to will do.

> "To read well, that is, to read true books in a true spirit, is a noble exercise, and one that will task the reader more than any other exercise which the customs of the day esteem."
> —Henry David Thoreau

I enjoy reading in the evenings after all the chores are done. It is nice to just sit quietly and reflect on the author's words and thoughts without being bothered by inane TV (though I do love my sitcoms—especially *The Big Bang Theory*), traffic horns, or unwelcome guests.

The Mountain Muse Is Upon Me and I Philosophize

As the evening creeps into the valley below I'm transfixed by the sun as it slowly slips behind the mountains to the west, transforming the sky into a kind of dazzling kaleidoscope of blues and golds, yellows and reds. If the evening should be cloudy I'm treated to the vision of brilliant crimson flashes spiraling through the clouds. What could be more beautiful? It's food for the soul. On clear nights I sit outside and gaze up at the stars and wonder; how many of the Earth's inhabitants have ever had the luxury of viewing the night sky—without the light pollution? It should a pre-requisite for the next day of your life for every Earthly being. On a really clear night you can see the milky way spreading itself across the night sky. It's then you begin to realize just how small and insignificant we really are on this miniscule planet. The universe, and its space co-dwellers is so vast and complex that I can't even wrap my head around it. It's improbable to believe that we on planet Earth are the only living things out there in the cosmos. My mind is stymied by the absurd futility of the warring, the strife, the hostilities that we have allowed and tolerated to evolve upon our tiny sphere. Are we but a cosmic anthill spinning around a blazing star, whirling through an inconceivable vastness of space? These are the thoughts I foster up here on my mountain—after twilight—under the stars. I don't get lonely. I relish the solitude. I enjoy going about my life neither a bother nor bothering. I'm done with the conflicts and dramas. Here in solitude I can delve into the mysteries of the universe, and perhaps even find out just what I am made of. Here I have found peace though some ghosts still haunt me, and they probably always will. But here on my mountain they are at least relegated to the deep recesses of my psyche where I can choose to ignore them or vanquish them altogether.

"The universe is wider than our views of it."
—Henry David Thoreau

Some of my friends have asked me if I ever get lonely up here all by myself. The answer is not just no. But hell no! I enjoy the solitude, and if I really have the need to talk to someone, besides Kiyo, I go down to Ernest T's, sit at his kitchen table, drink coffee and chat. Or—I can head further on down the mountain to Larry and Moe's for coffee and partake of whatever delectable concoction Moe has cooked up.

Tonight the setting sun is painting the northern sky salmon pink. Wispy clouds drift past my door. Smoke from the chimney wafts beyond my front window on its way down into the valley. The only sounds are the sputtering of boiling hotdogs and an occasional pinging of the sparks in the wood stove. I turn the damper down. Kiyo has been fed, though he looks at me like he wants some of what I'm having. Later he will curl up on the bed (sans) couch, which never seems to get folded back up into a couch these days. I can't see the point of folding it up when it's just me and Kiyo. I get little company way up here in the clouds.

> "I had three chairs in my house; one for solitude, two for friendship, three for society."
> —Henry David Thoreau

With the arrival of the nighttime, the cold air sweeps in, ushering in the impending hours of darkness. It's calm now, the brutal winds of last weekend have exited, leaving the mountain quiet and serene once again. The occasional drone of a plane flying into one of the airports below in St. Maries breaks the silence. Sometimes a logging truck headed home late for its unloading mission can be heard in the distance. But nothing else stirs. I just gave the fire a little poke, added another log, and opened up the damper for just a moment to chase off the night chill. It's still early, not yet time for bed, so I continue to sit and enjoy my book. These are the nights I most relish—a good fire—a good dog—and a good book. Tomorrow I'll split some more wood- after I dig it out from under a foot of new snow. I wanted to have all the wood split by now but other things have a way of intruding into my life, so now I must dig out frozen logs.

Do I get lonely up here? Again—not just no—but hell no!

> "Books are the carriers of civilization. Without books, history is silent, literature dumb, science crippled, thought and speculation at a standstill."
> —Henry David Thoreau

17

If the snow holds off next month, I think I will start working on Ancient Agatha. She's going to need a lot more work than I originally thought, but once she's finished she'll be a welcome addition to my little home. Come summer I'll probably have to invest in a small sandblaster and apply it lustily to this black beauty to free up some heavily rusted parts so I can get at the broken ones deep within her innards. If I can find someone online that can help me with parts and repairs things will go smoother. But fortunately *I know a guy* locally that is a wizard with a welder (I think he could weld air if he had to.). He just might be able to work some magic on the old girl. You can never *know too many guys.*

Damn! I have a leak in the transmission of my pickup. To fix it I will have to take the grill off, because that is where the leak is, lurking inside a small transmission cooler attached to the front of the radiator. This could turn out to be an all day project. I will have to take it down to Larry's place because he has all the tools I need, plus there is no snow at the foot of the mountain, so I won't get soaked to the skin while working on it. Oh the joys of owning an old truck. But she's been a good girl so I don't mind putting a little time into her.

The old guy I was getting wood from was asking after me last week. Seems he has more wood now that he wants to get rid of and he was wondering if I wanted some. Guess I made quite an impression on the old guy. Probably because he thinks I'm crazy to live on a mountaintop. He's a nice old fella', in his late 80s or early 90s. He's having his land logged off and selling the wood to a local mill. The profits from this will provide him with fuel and other essentials for the next few years. As the loggers cut, they cut off the ends (butts) and the tops because the marketable logs have to be a certain dimension and a certain length or the mill will not take them. So the old guy is left with all the waste, and the only other alternative (if he can't sell them to folks like me) is to burn them up. Huge waste. I'd love to take advantage of his offer but getting up to his place in the winter is just as hard as getting up to mine.

He too lives on the side of a mountain and though he and the loggers keep the road to his place pretty well open, it still would require me to chain up. And then once I have the load on my truck there is no way to get it up to my place. I would have to dump the load at Ernest T's or Larry's place and tote them up in small amounts by snowmobile. That would mean a hellofa lot of trips. I can't imagine delivering a pickup's worth of logs up to my place via dogsled. And I'm not even sure I want to go after more wood. I think I may have enough, though it would be nice to have a surplus—just in case. Maybe next week, if the weather holds, I'll give it a bit more thought. The wood would still be "green" and I would have to set them aside to dry out before I could burn them.

I have to explain—or rather clarify—my particular approach to wood chopping, just in case the reader is laboring under the misconception that I'm a non-stop dynamo with the ax and maul. In reality this is my routine: I chop a log—then throw a stick or piece of bark for Kiyo. He'll chase it—sometime bringing it back to me and sometimes leaving it where it landed. Before the last snowfall my driveway was littered with pieces of bark he left behind as he tired of the game. So it's chop, throw, chop, throw, repeat. It doesn't get much wood chopped but we do have fun. And it's a 'trip' to watch his face. He has so many expressions and sometimes the look of anticipation, the sparkle in his eyes, and the way he paws at my leg if I don't throw fast enough to suit him, just warms my heart. He has gotten used to this place and when I'm outside with him he wanders around checking things out. I'd like to believe any predators in my neighborhood have moved down the mountain following the game as it moves into a less robust clime. However, I still keep my eyes open and my gun handy just in case. I will really have to be on the alert this spring when the bears come out of their long winters nap. Don't want Kiyo getting between a mother bear and her cubs.

For the first six years of Kiyo's life he hasn't known anything but the inside of the cab of a truck—until this stint on the mountain. It's been an adjustment for him—getting used to being in one place for an extended spell—and not be constantly on the go. He now wakes up every morning excited and anxious to be let outside—to inspect his expansive new world. After that he pesters me 'til I feed him—then settles down for a bit until I start putting on my boots and coat. That sends him into a barking and jumping frenzy as he's come to realize this act means an outdoor frolic with me as the ringmaster.

He got hit by a chunk of flying wood the other day that flew off my chopping block. I tell him to watch out but sometimes he gets right in the way. Now when I say "watch out" he scuttles out of range of me and the log. If he sees me lifting the splitting maul he's clued into staying far back as well. He'll sit and wait until I swing—then he'll approach and start barking for me to throw a stick. Smart little dog. He quickly learned the meaning of the words "watch out"—and he does.

18

Ole' Man Winter—Bring It On!

> "In wildness is the preservation of the world."
> —Henry David Thoreau

The mountain is quiet now. We're into November and winter has claimed His sovereignty. The squirrels and chipmunks are bedded down in their warm little hidey-holes. Though sometimes, if the day warms up a bit, they peek out briefly and angrily scold me as I continue to cut and stack my firewood. Chickadees visited me twice now, and welcomed my promise to bring them chickadee-sustenance. They are cheery—and cheeky—little guys those presence always brightens my day. Crows are everywhere, and if I'm very lucky I occasionally spot a hawk or two, or spy a bald eagle soaring lazily on the up-drafts far in the distance.

Mornings often reveal fresh tracks encircling the cabin, left behind by some resident moose, or an occasional deer, most likely checking out this interloper—me! Then there are those tracks from the *others—the hunters*, hungrily stalking throughout the long cold nights—seeking a meal. I hear them sometimes—Kiyo seems most attuned to their presence—but I rarely see them. It's mostly their tracks that I see, or the remains of some poor beasty that abided on a lower rung of the food chain, lessening my forest neighborhood population by one. Sad.

The trees in this cold clime sway in the wind, dancing the dance of ancient rhythms, shedding the snow that may still cling to their branches. Most of the trees around the my abode are pine, though there are a few cedars sprinkled about. I have seen little evidence of red fir nearby, though I'm aware of their presence on this mountain as Ernest T and I have found a few.

> "...a taste for the beautiful is most cultivated out of doors...."
> —Henry David Thoreau

Sometimes It's Just About the Coffee

Progress, always progress. Just the smallest step forward brings a burst of encouragement propelling me ever onward and upward. My latest accomplishment? My acquisition of a new coffee maker. Now, instead of waiting for my wood stove to reach an acceptable temperature—red-hot apparently—to kick my percolator into action, I have a new drip coffee maker made by Coleman. This little beauty functions exceedingly well on my kitchen gas range—the one pulled out of the Casa del Fifth Wheel—yeah—I finally got the dang thing all hooked up. Now with a quick click to light the gas burner, in record time it provides me with my morning coffee—before the sun sets over the yardarm. (I propose the following theory: Farmers of yore got up before the crack of dawn because of the many hours it took for their woodstoves to heat their morning brew. Maybe, if all things functioned as they outta, it might be ready when they returned from the morning's milking. Don't know how true this theory might be, but up here alone on my mountain my brain can imagine almost anything.) The gas range is a bit slower than one that would operate on 110 volts, but it is certainly light-years faster than my wood-burner. Have to watch it closely though for once it has finished perking I have to be quick to turn off the gas—or settle for burnt coffee. Once perked I simply transfer it into the old coffee pot and settle it on the wood stove to keep warm throughout the morning. All this works just fine, and I no longer have to chew my last cup of coffee.

"Things do not change; we change."
—Henry David Thoreau

An Added Challenge

Don't want to dwell on it but my disabilities are a factor in facing life up here at Chez Walden. I must now practice the art of pacing myself. Tasks that might have taken me a couple of hours to complete back in the day, may now take me the better part of two days. But as the ole' tortoise says, "slow and steady wins the race." I now chart my work schedule in smaller increments as the muscles in my hands and feet cannot take a sustained strain. Oddly enough though, I have noticed that if I forget my medication—and I do when I get busy on a project—the pain of the neuropathy is minimal, albeit the muscles still remain weak. Pounding nails and chopping wood is harder than it should be and if I push too hard my hands simply poop out and let fling whatever happens to be in my hands. I've lost hammers in mid-swing and had to chase them down, and my splitting maul has flown halfway down the driveway on more than one occasion. My left hand is weaker than my right thanks to a TIA I suffered last December, and that—coupled with the myopathy in my hands and feet, can make simple tasks like chopping wood and pounding nails a bit of a challenge. The cold weather also plays a role for it further compromises the effects of this malady on my both hands and feet making it doubly difficult to hold onto tools and sustain a prolonged work effort.

I know it's time to call it a day when my hands will not hold the maul anymore and just before my left hand gives out entirely. If I continue to push myself, things begin flinging off into space or simply plunge to the ground. I have broken a few cell phones this way when I didn't realized that my hands had "let go" until the phone hit the floor. So I pace myself—doing hard physical labor for just a few hours at a go. I take many breaks:

1. Because I can!
2. To give my hands and feet a chance to recoup (and warm up).

However, I'm told it's good for me to pursue physical activity, to keep pushing myself, for it will slow the progress of this pain-in-the-butt disability, and help me retain the use of all my appendages longer. Good to know. I can never hope to be 100% again but I can slow the progress and keep body and soul from deteriorating.

Kiyo has learned to dodge many a flung maul or an air-bound hammer up here at Chez Walden. I think he understands that it wasn't intentionally aimed at him. Leastwise he readily forgives my faux pas once I ply him a few of his favorite treats.

So bring it on, *ole' man Winter*. You've got an old Navy Man here and a damn good dog beside him.

Thanksgiving Extraordinaire

Thanksgiving Day. Alone at Chez Walden. My most recent Thanksgiving memories were less then pleasant—either spending them on the road and noshing on a Turkey dinner ala truck stop, or worse, being at home among those whose whole objective seemed bent on making my life miserable. I'd planned to stoke the fire, settle in with a good book, and share a turkey leg with Kiyo. Then good neighbors and friends, Larry and Moe extended an invitation for me to join with them, and their family, for a good old-fashioned Thanksgiving Dinner. Now Moe may be one of the best darn cooks I've even come across so it didn't take but a minute to for me to accept their invitation. I eagerly navigated down the mountainside to their gracious home with a bottle of good Blackberry wine in tow. I'd forgotten the fun a family can have together. Their sons were there along with their wives. We laughed, dined on scrumptious turkey with all the fixings, told jokes, consumed more food, laughed some more, drank Blackberry wine, and shared a few more jokes. Moe's cooking was something you only dream about (sorry Ma). But it was the fun of a functional family celebrating the joy of being together. Moe and I finished off the wine before evening settled in. Then, before I left to wind my way back up the mountainside Moe loaded me up with slabs of pie, cookies, spinach dip and fancy breads for dipping. What a great day. If I couldn't be back East with my Mom, sister and her family then this was certainly the next best thing. I went home full of laughter, full of great vittles, maybe just a little too much wine, and fell into bed as soon as I coaxed the fire into a steady burn.

Things I am thankful for this Thanksgiving:

I have a cabin with no electricity, *but I have a cabin.*

I drain my sink into a bucket because I have no drain to the outside, *but I have a sink—and a bucket.*

I heat with wood and sometimes it's chilly inside, *but I have wood and heat.*

I have no running water and no well, *but I have good neighbors that let me get water from their well.*

I do not yet have enough electrical power to run my refrigerator, *but it is cold outside so my food stays chilled.*

Sometimes it is hard making it up the mountain because of the weather, *but I have tire chains, a good truck, and a snowmobile if that is the only way up.*

I have good friends close by in case I need them or they need me.

I have peace of mind, body and soul, which is something I haven't had in years.

I could go on forever about things now in my life that I am thankful for: *the trees, the wildlife, the quiet.*

I am thankful for the shear joy of being alive. After everything I have been through this past year *I am now truly at peace.*

> "I am grateful for what I am and have. My thanksgiving is perpetual. It is surprising how contented one can be with nothing definite—only a sense of existence."
> —Henry David Thoreau

19

Damn! Canada Again!

Another load to Canada. Ontario to be precise. It was two weeks before the Christmas holidays and I really didn't want this damn load, and my instincts proved right. It proved to be one of the most frustrating and annoying runs I've ever been under. First it was presented as a legal load—meaning size and weight were in acceptable limits. But when I arrived at the yard and took one look at the paperwork it was obviously an oversize load. That changed everything. It had been scheduled for the wrong-size trailer, thus delaying departure for three days. The shipper couldn't seem to understand that you can't load 57 feet of freight onto a 48 foot trailer. That snafu, and getting all minds on the same page, delayed the whole process by another full day. Finally on the road, I assumed it would be smooth sailing. Not so. When I got to the border of Canada it was discovered that I didn't have the proper permit to enter the country with an oversize load. Another delay of a full 48 hours before that dilemma was resolved. Finally I arrived at our Canadian destination. (here Murphy's Law *really* kicks in) The receivers took a full day to unload me, then another full day to reload with the returning freight. It seemed an eternity before I arrived back on native soil. But I wasn't done yet. I had more freight to load in Indiana and Illinois. After another full day of loading I drove on to Walcott, Iowa before crashing for the night. This trip had been trouble, with a capital T, from beginning to end. Bad snow storms and slick roads caused a delay for two more days in South Dakota and Montana. Then I got pulled into a scale in Butte, Montana for a paperwork check. Though these checks are usually exasperating, often demanding and overly picky, this one turned out to be something of a perk. The DOT Officer checking my logbook asked if I realized I had gone over the 14-hour rule—this on the day I had actually been in a holding pattern while being loaded. This offence usually results in a ticket and hefty fine. I responded with an apology—told him I had not realized it and I was sorry. He looked at me and said "Are you human?" (strange?) Well, of course I said "yes."

Then he replied, "Well, humans make mistakes. The rest of your logs are correct so I'm going to overlook this." To say I was shocked is an understatement. This is not typical behavior for a DOT cop. With nasty business behind us, we somehow fell into chatting about cabins and such. I told him I was retired, only taking Canada loads, and couldn't wait to get back to my mountain home. He lit up, smiled and shared that he too had a remote wilderness cabin. It was in Wyoming and accessible in the winter only by a fifteen-mile jaunt on a snowmobile. He continued describing how he had just finished insulating, putting on a new roof and painting his backwoods' retreat. I shared my resolve to live off the grid but when I related my plans to house the batteries for the solar system in an old truck body I'd hauled up the mountain for that purpose, he shook his head. He admonished me that I was inviting trouble. They would freeze, he cautioned, in an unheated environment. He suggested that I might want to consider digging an old-fashion root cellar instead. Underground, the temperature would stay constant and the batteries wouldn't freeze. I hadn't considered this possibility and his option struck me as a hellofa good idea. We could have talked the night away but I had to get a move on. Serendipitous interactions with folks like that cop make life on the road bearable—even pleasant—renewing my faith in human nature, generating good vibes, and swaddling my world with positive energy.

Guess this Summer I'll Be Digging a Root Cellar.

In my absence Larry and Moe agreed to stow my firearms for me. We all felt it was wisest not to leave them at the cabin while no one was there. Not only did they offer this for me but Moe suggested I bring her all my dirty dishes (these included everything I had dirtied myself as well as those stored in Casa del Fifth Wheel—which I knew mice and chipmunks had tapped-danced over). OMG What great neighbors! Additionally in my absence Moe bought thermal sheets for my bed and thermal drapes for my windows. Meanwhile, my Mom sent me another care-package from Florida which included military issue thermal underwear and more cozy bedding. Gosh. 'Ya gotta love the women in my life.

Doodlebugs and Stuff

Doodlebug tractor is the colloquial American English name for a home-made tractor made in the United States during World War II when production tractors were in short supply. The Doodlebug of the 1940s was usually based on a 1920s or 1930s era Ford automobile which was then modified either by the complete removal or alteration of some of the vehicle's body. The preservation of examples of the Doodlebug tractor has become popular in New England and upstate New York where clubs hold monthly meet-ups in the summer months to put their contraptions to the test by pulling large stone boats in a tractor pull.

Years ago as a kid growing up in the foothills of the White Mountains of New Hampshire my family would often embark on weekend trips through the back roads and the farm country of the bucolic states of northern New England. On these trips I often spied curious old model T's forlornly rusting away in some old farmer's field, out behind his barn, or sometimes sheltered under a shed overhang. I later learned these old-timey vehicles were slated to be converted into tractors by their Yankees owners. Gotta love that Yankee ingenuity. Well, by now you have ascertained that I love anything old—and all things mechanical. If I could have been turned loose on one of these old machines I would have been in heaven. But at that time my family hadn't the appropriate facilities for such a venture so it was not to be.

I also remember an old Yankee who lived just down the road from my parent's home in the village of Wakefield, New Hampshire. He had a fenced-in pasture behind his barn that was a veritable garden of old model A's and T's. Each Fall, just before the first snowfall, he would drag one of those darlin's into his barn and by the following Spring it would reappear, spit-shined, and polished, totally revamped and looking brand new again. As a kid I walked through his "garden" many a time, lusting after those wanton relics and dreaming of what I might do if ever I got my hands on one. As a kid I knew neither the history, nor the purpose, of one particular relic that sat rusting away in his pasture. I only knew I wanted it. I now know it was a "doodlebug."

Now fast forward a bunch of years. I own an old 1965 Chevy 3/4 ton pickup. I bought it from a friend a few years back when I was still in the Naval Reserves to use as transportation to and from drill weekends, instead of having to drive my rig. Curiously enough throughout the long, bitter divorce, (though I'll never know why) it became legal fodder—ownership disputed—possession fought over—the heated wrangling went on for months. In the end this poor 'ole broken-down chariot remained mine, and here it sits at my Chez Walden estate, un-used, under-loved and seriously in need of a full body restoration—which currently I have neither the time or the money for. *But I do need a tractor.* Slowly and steadily an idea seeped into my brain as I recalled the old model T's of those bygone pastures. Staring me in the face, wallowing at my backdoor, waits my very own Doodlebug.

She isn't the right vintage but she has the right "stuff." I think I can make most of the conversions myself—though maybe not the two gear boxes—that will require another transmission and a bit more labor than I think I want to indulge in. But she has a positive track rear-end, meaning both axles drive the truck, instead of just one. I think with the right approach and with expertise of my many mechanically talented friends I just may be able to get a workable tractor out of her. I will add some sort of rig to her frame, similar to that of a tow truck, and maybe add a winch to her front-end for dragging logs out of the woods. But of greater significance, she'll support a plow and will have the guts to keep my access road open in the winter months. I see a Doodlebug tractor in my future.

A Future Doodlebug?

"It's not what you look at that matters, it's what you see."
—Henry David Thoreau

Ernest T and Sherylee have decided to stay here and plan to tough-it-out through the winter. As promised, Ernest T re-vamped his marvelous drag apparatus and we have high-hopes that this heftier and gutsier version will do the job—that is, keep our road open—and keep us on the mountain. In mid-November we experienced a bit of warm weather causing the packed road-snow to melt. Ernest T took advantage of this condition and towed his drag up to my place, in anticipation of the snowstorms prophesied to descend upon us later this week. With the drag at my place we plan to prepare that stretch of road with a good pre-storm scrapping. There is no doubt we face a challenge in keeping the quarter mile s-curve from his place to mine open and passable.

This winter's *Plan A* is to be able to drive my truck right to my doorstep all winter long.

Plan B is to park my pick-up at his place and complete the trip via snowmobile. We hope the heavier drag he devised will do the job so I won't have to resort to *Plan B*.

So now comes the downhill prep. Both of Ernest T's trucks have diesel motors producing a heck of a lot more horsepower than my gas motored vehicle. My pickup with drag in tow easily made a clean sweep down the mountainside, but on the return trip I was only able to haul it as far up as Ernest T's driveway. The thing is just too darn heavy for my light-weight truck. Ernest T! It's all up to you! Keep me on the mountainside.

While Ernest T was here he helped me tote the fridge from Casa del Fifth Wheel into the cabin. Been wanting to do that for a while. It was the last important item to rip from her loins. Can't use it yet—not until I get set up with electrical power, but I sure can get it cleaned up and ready. So, once I finished my allotted wood-chopping for the day, I heated up some water on the wood stove and scrubbed it, inside and out. While I was at it, I decided to scrub up the Maytag as well. Now these two beauties sit, ready, willing and able to do my bidding just as soon as I can throw the switch. It will sure be nice, not having to drive into town to do laundry.

My Beauty #1.

My Beauty #2.

20

It's been snowing here off and on all day, though the stuff is light and hasn't accumulated much more than an inch on the ground. It's as though Ole' Man Winter is sending out advance troupes to test neighborhood. I plan to wait until it gets a little deeper before dragging the road. No sense wasting gas for an inch of snow. It was predicted that we would see five to six inches of the stuff today. I think the storm is still north of us; maybe planning a midnight assault. Weather is so hard to predict up here on the mountain. Thus far it has been a mild winter, but we've barely into it and have a few more solid months of winter to get through. Already I'm beginning to look forward to spring when I can turn my attention to some of my more ambitious outdoor projects.

Well, He Brought It On!

Well, He Brought It On!

'Ole man has finally arrived in full battle armor. He summoned forth two huge back to back snow storms leaving my pick-up virtuously immobilized—buried, surrounded, and topped off with eighteen inches of the heavy white stuff. The winds accompanying these storms were vicious, causing small mountains to appear in my yard where just two days ago there was level ground. I scratch my head and wonder if I'll ever be able to get out of my driveway, and—if I do manage to get out, will I be able to get back in? Maybe not 'til spring melt-off. I don't like that idea one little bit. I need my snowmobile. I need to pack in a few months supplies of food and water. If that becomes an impossibility then I will have to abandon my utopia until sometime in March. This is definitely not what I had planned. This is my home of choice and I don't want to leave it. But on the other hand I don't want to starve to death here either. Kiyo looks concerned.

Yeah. I would absolutely hate having to leave here. It would not bode well with me if the weather should force me off the mountain. I would worry about this place without me here to defend and protect it. There is so much still to be done on this property and I lost so much time those days when I was sick. And then there was that load from hell into Ontario and back that really put me behind. I will do what I must to survive. If I am forced to leave until spring I can only hope to find this place hale and hearty, and still in good order upon my return.

As I contemplate my options I marvel at the nearby trees as they perform their winter dance, flinging great waves of snow from their limbs and branches, and slamming them onto my cabin's roof. This snow is so heavy I'm surprised my cabin can hold up under its barrage. It seems impervious to the assault. I'm equally surprise that the trees themselves, along with their laden boughs, haven't cracked and shattered.

After the storms abated Ernest T pulled his drag up to my place and together we managed to clear a good bit of snow from the road between his place and mine. I'm concerned though.

All the banks of snow piled along its edges are building up too fast and too high. Without some melting and rotting away of these bankings, we simply will not have any place to push future accumulations, and that could spell a big problem. We did a pretty good job of clearing the road going down the mountain but on the return trip we could only get the drag back up as far as Ernest T's driveway—not mine. A bad indicator. If we can't haul this drag up to my place then the option of getting my truck up the mountain beyond Ernst's driveway is pretty nil.

And if the snow gets much deeper—and it will—I might not even be able to get in and out by snowmobile. A snowmobile requires a packed trail, and what do I pack it with?

The Return of My Snowmobile.

My snowmobile has been in the shop these past weeks getting a couple of glitches fixed and preparing it for the tough months ahead. Finally I have it back. And just in time! The cost to repair it was surprisingly less than I thought it would be, though the time it took seemed in the extreme. I guess I can be happy with the tradeoff. Ernest T fired up his snow machine and together we took off for a trial run up and down the mountain road—from his place to mine. She performed just fine. It passed the test and I believe it will be a good little machine to have up here to serve my needs. I got it back not a minute too soon; full-blown winter is hovering around my doorstep.

Snow, Snow, and a Snowmobile in Wait.

The concerns regarding our ability to keep the road open for our ease of access grow by the day. After turning off from the main road and heading up the mountain trail the way gets a bit 'hairy'. The road between Ernest T's place and mine is fast becoming a conundrum. Will it remain passable—an s-curve on a steep incline? I'm rethinking *Plan B* and will probably initiate *Plan C*—that being leaving *both* my truck *and* snowmobile at the bottom of the mountain at Larry and Moe's place. That plan affords me the luxury of not having the onerous task of continually putting chains on and off my pick-up based on whether I'm climbing up the mountain, or crawling back down into town, and on paved roads. With my snowmobile at Larry and Moe's I have a chance (hopefully) to haul myself and my supplies, if not all the way to my place, at least to Ernest T's. It will be a challenge to lug everything up from there but better then getting my truck stuck half-way up the mountain for the duration of the winter. Now I just have to contrive a way to effectively hookup the dog sled to its hind end.

With the onset of winter things here seem at a standstill. I chop wood. Everything else has been put on hold until spring. I have pretty much made a final decision about my addition. It will indeed be an ell. Also contemplating burying the truck body under the proposed addition, thereby creating an instant root cellar. This seems a good solution for the storage of the batteries. As the DOT Cop told me, they won't freeze underground. With things on a winter hiatus—I stoke the fire, read books, chop wood, and reflect on spring. Also, since my addition will be an ell, I am considering making the ground level my bedroom, and instead of an open loft above I will entirely close off the ceiling and use it for storage space. That will give me an office, a bedroom, with the bathroom still situated behind the kitchen, affording more efficiency in the running of water pipes.

Creaks and Groans

Can it be? Am I getting to old for some of this stuff? I've chopped wood for two days and now my body is talking back. Pain. My back aches, my head hurts, I just hurt all over. Decision made. *Next year I will invest in a gas-powered wood splitter.* Just push a button and *poof,* it's done! Or maybe I'll just have the wood brought to me already cut and split, then all I'll have to do is stack it. Ahhh, the brilliance of ideas when you're alone on a mountaintop. I may even consider buying a whole logging truck load of wood, if the price is right, then all I'll have to do is cut and split it as needed. Still, a gas powered splitter would be a fine toy to have. A few other toys I want to consider before next winter: a plow, a bigger truck with a diesel motor, a snow blower, more and bigger batteries, and a wind turbine or two would be nice.

21

> "I have struck a chord,
> It's a girl, my lord,
> Slowing down to take a look at me!"
> —(Very loosely borrowed from the eagles "take it easy")

I promised myself, and all those around me, that I would *never* allow myself to get romantically involved with another woman. I'd picked poorly twice now and each one had left me poorer, both emotionally and financially. Read on.

It has long been a credo in my family that a heightened sense of humor is the barometer of true intelligence. It's not the degree one holds, or the years—or lack thereof—of formal schooling that accounts for a person's I.Q. It's the humorous insight and fun they bring to the party. "Most people are educated beyond their intelligence" is an oft-used phrase quoted by my Mom. She's right. I married two women whose sense of humor mirrored that of a sloth on a cold day. They didn't understand my oft-times perverted humor, and absolutely loathed my family for the laughter and fun they brought to the table. I realize now that their hatred most-likely stemmed from unspoken, even unrecognized, feelings of inadequacy and intimidation when, during those brief few times they were in the company of my Mom and sister, they sat mute while we all doubled over in laughter. As I stated earlier, my family laughs a lot and love to 'rag' on one another. The lack of that laughter-quotient in my spouses was a contributing factor to the erosion of both my marriages.

Well. Now fast forward to the recent entrance of Tracy into my life.

I met my gal Tracy on one of those dating web sites. It's one of the better ones, and she was a "what if" on my site that I almost passed up. Honestly, I was just fishin' around, with no real intention of getting involved with another women. I was happy single and alone with just my puppy on my mountaintop. But lucky for me I made a last-minute decision and responded to her questions. It turned out to be the best call I ever made, for she is the female half of me. She's the yin to my yang. We share the same likes in movies and TV (the Big Bang Theory is our absolute favorite); the same taste in wine and food, the same outrageous sense of humor, and we even tend to know what the other one is thinking, frequently sending mirroring texts to each other. ("Get outta my head," we joke.) We finish each other's sentences, but more importantly we laugh long and often and find mutual fun in the most absurd situations.

Now here's the problem—Tracy lives in Edmonton, Alberta, Canada and works the Canadian Oil Sands Projects, nearly five hundred miles to the north. Her company flies her in to that desolate location for ten-days stints, and then flies her back home for a four-day reprieve. She loves her job—gets to meet the most interesting people (even a few "Ice Truckers" featured on the T.V. program of the same name) and is very comfortably compensated. Obviously the logistics of a courtship from two abutting countries is vastly complicated. After months of rewarding on-line communication I decided to take the bull by the horns and drive up to meet her at a resort near her home-base. It was the first time we laid eyes on each other, and we 'clicked' immediately. In fact our cosmic-attraction was so strong that following the two-day resort stay (with two days left of her four days off) she invited me to her home—a sweet little condo- and to met her family. Her mom, dad, she and I shared a scrumcious meal together and—like my family—her's laughed a lot too, and at the same absurd things that tinkle our funny bones. I managed to win her dad's 'stamp of approval'. I'm told that's hard to come by.

The Mark of a Tough Gal

She was intrigued by my existence on a mountaintop. She couldn't wait to see it for herself. So we made another date. One a few months hence. She was to fly here and spend a weekend at Chez Walden. I warned her things were still in a pretty rough state. No soft-plushy living at my casa. No room service. No gourmet meals. *No flush toilet*. She couldn't wait. When finally the day came to introduce her to my forested abode she was hooked.

My sister, from her plush, comfortable surroundings in Florida queried, "What kind of girl have you got now that is willing to pee in a bucket?"

"A Canadian girl." I replied.

Tracy loved the place at first sight and can't wait to see it finished. We made plans for a return visit right after Christmas.

Now both of us are independent people who really don't *need* someone in our lives. We feel complete just as we are. However, both of us *want* someone in our lives. Someone to enhance the person we already are and to share the joys. We want someone to laugh with. I joke that now that I have a summer place here, I could have a winter place up north. (Of course the idea is ludicrous. Who would want to winter in Alberta?)

> "Love must be as much a light, as it is a flame.
> —Henry David Thoreau

Just days before Christmas I lost my brakes as I was traveling up the mountain. One of the rear brake lines must have rusted and just pooped out. The next morning was the 24th of December so I had to get it fixed immediately or I would be stuck without a vehicle until after the holiday. This simply would not do because Tracy was flying in from Canada on the 26th to spend a late-Christmas sojourn with me at Chez Walden. On our mountaintop we'd just had an unseasonable warm spell—turning all the snow into slush. Ernest T had dragged the road earlier the day before but by nightfall everything froze solid and the road became a rutted mess of ice—from top to bottom. Now this turn of events was seriously going to compound my problem. Have I mentioned that I have to chain up every time I take this mountain trek? Fortunately I had all four chains on so I decided to give it a go. I had to get down the mountain and fix this darn thing. I put the truck in low gear and slowly, ever so slowly, headed down. The first part of the trip was not too bad. The ruts from past thawing and freezing cycles actually helped keep my truck from picking up too much speed. But as I descended further down the mountain it became a little hairy. As I approached one of the turns I spooked a big bull moose. Fortunately, for both him and me, he bolted off the road and lumbered into the woods. On the very next turn I spun completely around finally stopping with the truck's rear-end facing downhill. Not good. I was beginning to perspire. I finally managed to get it turned about with front end facing properly downhill again. With much cussing and gritting of teeth I started the slow drive back down again. After what seemed an eternity, and a few hundred miles—not the mile and a half it is—I made it to the bottom. I got to Larry's just before they were about to leave for town. The first piece of luck today. He drove me to the local auto parts store where I was informed that they needed to see the old brake line so they could match it for length. So a quick jaunt back to Larry's and I hastily pulled off the old line. Another quick trip into town and I had the appropriate part plus two quarts of brake fluid. With Larry's help and his enclosed workshop we got the new line installed and bled, and I had my old girl back up and running before noon. Tracy darlin'—I'll be able to pick you up at the airport.

St. Nick Brings a Bag-Full of Joy

Christmas was gonna be a hard time for me. It rekindles memories of that medivac flight out of Kuwait. Compound that ache with the hatefulness of the past twelve months and I simply didn't have the heart to commemorate the season. I hadn't planned on putting up a tree, or celebrating in any way at all, that is until Tracy announced the far-off date we'd planned was at hand and her flight was scheduled to arrive here the day after Christmas. So when Ernest T stopped by just before the holidays offering me the scraggly top he had lopped off a red fir (he had an identical one for his own family), I decided to stick it in a pot and decorate it. Appreciative though I was of Ernest T's neighborly gesture this poor 'ole tree made Charlie Brown's look lush and full-bodied by comparison.

Curiously enough, the box of Christmas decorations my Mom had given me years ago—most with special significance from my childhood—had appeared on the doorstep of Casa del Fifth Wheel just after the divorce. I had never expected to see them again. Savoring each one as it emerged from the box I nostalgically attached these relics, one by one, upon the sparse boughs of my 'first' Chez Walden Christmas tree.

Tracy, knowing all that I had been through, was eager to create some happy memories for me this year. This was our third date and our first Christmas together. Even still, I was struggling to get old memories out of my head. I don't think they will ever go away completely. However, true to her promise Tracy and I did make some great new ones together.

We did some cooking on the gas range, the first time that's been used since it was transplanted into the cabin. We cooked a small ham, and some corn and beans for a simple Christmas dinner. The next morning I prepared her a

My Own Charlie Brown Tree.

breakfast of ham and eggs, and served it to her in bed. That's something I don't think I have done in years. I fully enjoyed pampering her. It's amazing how much better everything tastes when you're in good company. Our simply pauper's fare seemed a luxurious banquet—fit for a King and his Queen.

Later in the day she helped me cut and stack wood, something that is always in need around here but much more fun with a pretty girl by my side.

Larry and Moe had earlier suggested that we might join them for a trek into the backlands to see the eagles. Apparently this is a yearly event of hundreds of bald eagles in migration and hundreds of spectators snapping pictures. They fly in to some of the nearby lakes for the kokanee, a land-locked Salmon that spans this time of year, before they die.

BAYVIEW, Idaho—December 2013 — Bayview residents say an abundance of spawning kokanee in their bay of Lake Pend Oreille have made this year's December eagle-watching season one to remember. The residents said the number of eagles this December is "tenfold" compared with past years. "Living in a post card," on. They attribute the eagle turnout to the strong comeback kokanee have made in Lake Pend Oreille. In 2013, for the first time since 1999, anglers were allowed to keep a limit of six kokanee from the lake. The kokanee also feed the lake's popular rainbow trout. The delicious fish's spawning activity in the bay has held the eagles' attention longer than most years, Jones said. The bay usually gets about 50 eagles, but this year it's in the hundreds. They feed on the kokanee as they migrate south, before turning around and heading back north in February to prepare for reproduction. So, as kokanee go, so go the eagles. The lake is so alive with the kokanee, an Audubon paradise with each tree "stacked" with five or six eagles. They can be heard talking, quibbling over space in a tree, using their distinctive calls. Dead kokanee can be seen scattered across the lake bottom, where it's visible. The fish die after spawning. A rare live one languidly swims by now and then along the bottom, looking half-dead like a zombie. Carrie Hugo, a U.S. Bureau of Land Management wildlife biologist, said she spotted 217 bald eagles along her regular 12-mile route along Lake Coeur d'Alene on Monday.

We visited two different lakes. One we were told usually had three-hundred or so eagles at it. We saw only five. Then we went for a late lunch before heading to lake Coeur d'Alene, at Wolf Bay. However, it was getting late in the day, the temperature was dropping, and the eagles had begun to bed down for the night. We didn't see all that the spectacular event promised, but we were able to snap a few really good pictures and we thoroughly enjoyed the adventure and the good company. Ahhh. We had begun to construct those new memories we had promised ourselves.

A Migrating Eagle in Flight.

Oh, and did I mention that my gal's pretty as well? and that she totally won over everyone in my world—even my mother from far-away sunny Florida was wowed with a box of Scottish shortbread cookies Tracy baked and mailed her (to the tune of $25.00 per/USPS).

"In her midst I can be glad with an entire gladness.
If this world were all man, I could not stretch myself,
I should lose all hope. He is restraint; she is freedom to me.
He makes me wish for another world; she makes me content with this.
None of the joys she supplies is subject to his rules and definitions.
What he touches he taints. In thought he moralizes...
How infinite and pure the least pleasure of which
Nature is basis compared with the congratulations of mankind!
The joy which Nature yields is like that afforded by frank
words of one we love."
—Henry David Thoreau

22

"Live each season as it passes; breathe the air, drink the drink, taste the fruit, and resign yourself to the influences of each."
—Henry David Thoreau

With the Holidays now in my rear-view mirror I've officially entered into the realm of the season of ice and snow and the true beginnings of my challenges upon the mountain with 'ole Man Winter. Will I have what it takes to make it? Only the days ahead will determine that. It's hard sometimes to believe it's January; the weather has been so mild throughout this month. I'm told that in a typical winter this part of the world would already be host to five-feet of snow on the ground. That would sure make getting up and down this mountain very difficult. Up 'til now we have had a yoyo weather pattern: first snow, then a thaw, then more snow, and thaw again, leaving us with just about eighteen inches of snow on the ground. For this I am glad because I'm not really as prepared as I'd hoped to be for weathering the winter months here. Not enough wood, no water, very little electricity, the list goes on. Next year however, I plan to be far better off and well prepared. We (my neighbors and I) have been given a grader to plow the road but as for this year neither Ernest T or myself have the time to tinker with it and get it up and running. This baby needs considerable welding done on the transmission case and her brakes need repairing. Come spring we will start work on it, and by next winter we should be able to keep the road open with ease. Even though Ernest T's drag has been doing a pretty good job thus far, it will not work much longer before the road will only become accessible by snowmobile.

Experiencing the Wilderness Up Close and Personal

I'm now traversing the last quarter mile to Chez Walden by snowmobile. My pickup is parked below at Ernest T's place. He's been able to keep the road clear up to his driveway, but neither his truck nor mine will pull the drag any further up the steep grade and hairpin turn to my place. So I'm guessing that for the duration of this winter I'll be experiencing the joys of roughing-it to get supplies up to my cabin. Ahhh, winter in the wilderness up close and personal, lugging all my necessities up by snowmobile and dog sled.

I wasn't able to rig up the dogsled exactly as I'd planned but what I have rigged up seems to work just fine. It's just a one-inch strap hooked from the rear of the snowmobile and attached to two hooks on the dogsled. When I got back from my last run into Coeur d'Alene I parked the truck at Ernest T's and transferred a few of my purchases onto the dogsled. A smallish load to start with, just a seven-gallon jug of water and the new generator. I revved up the snowmobile for her maiden supply run and headed her northward, but as I turned from the driveway onto the up-hill road toward Chez Walden I got stuck. There was not enough room to turn around and I ended up in deep snow and got buried—me, snowmobile, dogsled and all! After calling myself every stupid name in the book I finally got everything righted but then feared the dogsled might tip over on me while heading up the steep climb to the cabin. It didn't. I made two more trips from Ernest T's to Chez Walden and felt I was beginning to get the hang of this mini-rig—only tipping the dogsled once. Far different skills needed for this little baby than for my big rig.

I haven't been on a snowmobile since I was a kid, and that one I acquired for just $50 bucks! It was an old Moto-ski, with an air cooled one-cylinder engine and a metal gas tank. It was back in the 70s. Two of our neighbors owned brand new snow machines and their kids—my buddies Dean and Todd—were having a blast running up and down our dirt road, and throughout the network of nearby logging roads. My parent didn't see the need for us to own one, certainly not a brand new one, and no amount of whining could convince them otherwise. I felt deprived until the happy day one of my school chums told me he had an old machine for sale, and because he couldn't keep it running he wanted just $50.00 for it. It was older than anything my friends frolicked about upon, probably built in the late 50s or 60s, but I jumped at it, bought it, and my Dad and I quickly hauled it home. I soon discovered why it wouldn't stay running. This aged machine had a metal gas tank which had accumulated a good bit of rust within it's innards and it was being sucked into the carburetor, efficiently clogging it up. So to compensate, the team of Dean, Todd and myself strapped a one-gallon gas can in the space next to the foot rest and ran a hose up to the carburetor. Rube Goldberg though it may have been, the results were surprisingly efficient, and away I went joining my pals on wild winter escapades. This was freedom! No words can describe the fun of racing up a packed trail and over to nearby Moose Mountain to spend the afternoon skiing when you're just 15-years-old. It was not a fast machine, but on a trail it isn't speed that you need. I kept this machine until its final breakdown, just before I left for Naval Boot Camp. Then I sold it to one of the guys that worked at Moose Mountain. He paid $50.00 for it. I'd say I got my money's worth.

This new machine of mine has three cylinders, is liquid cooled—great for trail riding—and with enough power to pull my dogsled up the hill. *I haven't had so much fun in years.* The wind slapping at my face is cold, invigorating, but hardly worth noticing as I push the throttle and speed up the mountain trail. Yee Haw! Kiyo hates it as much as I love it and I have to buckle him to me or he will jump off. It makes it a little hard when I have to lean into a turn, but I'm learning. The dogsled is narrow so I'll engineer some kind of outriggers to keep it stable when negotiating some of the S-curves. This should prevent tip-over's and spilling precious cargo. Kiyo used to love riding on the 4-wheeler I once owned, but he's having second thoughts about riding this contraption. Don't know if it's the cold or the noise but I have to come up with some kind of secure design to keep him safe.

For now I must tie him in front of me and this is a problem because when I have to lean with the machine I just about drag him off. I'm thinking about a pouch of some kind that I can put him in and strap him over my shoulder. This will not only keep him from falling off but will also keep him snug and warm. Leaving him at the cabin would almost break his heart. He gets lonely when he's left for too long. Also—I would miss not having him near me. Hopefully he and I will work out a happy solution for I'm pretty certain Ernest T will not be able to keep the road open even up to his place for the duration of the winter. That will leave Kiyo and I riding this trail all the way up from Larry's—two miles. Now that's going to be fun. And challenging. And damn cold! But as long as

I can continue to truck food and water up here I'll be able to stay the winter and we will be just fine.

Larry is campaigning for a dozer. He and Ernest T are toying with the idea of purchasing an old military 6x6 truck (it's a six wheel drive truck) complete with a plow. In the midst of their plotting, Moe discovered an old snow cat offered online for $9,000 (or best offer). Now that would be my choice. Damn things can go anywhere with their wide tracks. Would never again have to worry about the road condition if we had one of those things. And think of the fun! It might also keep the recreational snowmobilers off our road once the snow gets too deep. Last weekend there were a number of four-wheelers whizzing past my cabin. Having a cleared road invites anyone up here—anytime. I don't like the thought of having to lock up my place, though I know I'll have to start come spring when I leave. I like the thought of not just anyone coming up whenever they feel like it. Yes—I enjoy my solitude. I want to deal with people on my own terms and not have them stumbling around up here, causing trouble. There is a property up above me that is gated off. The owner built a pole barn housing a trailer and a back hoe inside. It was broken into last year so I've gotta believe that some who come up this way have no good intentions.

I came upon a downed tree straddling the road today as I headed down to help Larry with his roof. He had just suggested yesterday that I should start carrying my chainsaw with me at all times. Is he physic? Nevertheless I left my chainsaw at home because my truck is now berthed at Ernest T's place, and with my ongoing need for a chainsaw at the cabin, I don't want to continually be hauling it back and forth from the truck to the snowmobile. Fortunately it was a small tree and I was able to push it aside with my truck.

23

Am I Crazy?

"Go confidently in the direction of your dreams. Live the life you have imagined."
—Henry David Thoreau

Sometimes I wonder if I'm sane—living up here. I will be fifty-three-years old this year and question if this adventure is something for a younger man. There was a time I wanted to move to Alaska, build a log cabin and live off the land, hunting and fishing. I was much younger then and could have borne the hardships much better at that age. But—I got married and the other half of that union wanted nothing to do with cold weather. So here I am in my 50s trying to stay warm—chop wood—keep what snow there is from building up on the roofs—get up and down off this mountain without killing myself, and on top of that I have this damn disability that slows me down.

Pulled a muscle in my shoulder yesterday, hurts like hell, getting older really sucks. Trying to take it easy today but needed to finish off the roof over the back room. Wanted to get the kitchen roof cleaned off too but I think it will have to wait a day or two. So taking it easy today.

This morning the fire was out, I stoked it up before bed as I normally do, and let it run for a minute with vent wide open, then shut everything down and went to bed. When I woke up at 5:30 it was out, the wood I put in last night still un-burnt and it's belly is stone-cold. I don't know what happened, but it was damn cold inside! I jumped up and got it going again but as of right now it's still damn chilly in here.

The little generator I picked up seems to be working fine, I fired it up to watch a movie and it did keep the batteries charged, though it's slower than using the truck. I will be glad when I can get the big generator up and running. That's going to take some work, as it looks like the oil filter has never been changed, so chances are the oil has never been changed either. Then I have to make new exhaust gaskets, as the local auto parts store didn't have anything to match the old ones. I will also have to change spark plugs, and put on a new hose for the air filter—run a gas line to the 80 gal. tank I have outside (with a fuel filter), and then figure out where to run the exhaust plus install a new muffler. I will have 110 volts then but I will have to run the wires above ground until spring. That's not entirely safe so a little worried about getting it up and running right now. Also, haven't got any gas in the tank so will have to figure out how to get enough gas up here to run it. Though I don't intend to run it very often I would like it to be functional so I can operate my Maytag and watch a little more TV. I can't wait until spring when I can really get things moving again around here at Chez Walden.

I want to build a frame around that old truck body and side over it to mirror the cabin's siding, so it will look like a real out building (guest house?). Also plan to attach a pitched roof on it to house my solar panels. It will get a lot more sun once Casa del Fifth Wheel is hauled out of here, for the snow piled upon it's roof now is currently blocking the sun's ray from the truck body. Next spring I will add a deck to extend the length of the east side of the cabin, with roof above, for ease of stacking fire wood and sheltered from snow and drifts before next winter.

> "What you get by achieving your goals is not as important as what you become by achieving your goals.
> —Henry David Thoreau

Doctor's orders—I'm not to use my left arm for two weeks. Seems I pulled some muscles in my shoulder last week chopping wood (what else?). I'm not going to enjoy this hiatus one small bit. The weather has been nice and I had hoped to get the rest of the wood split before the next snow. Eyeing what I have still un-split I'm guessing I probably have enough to get through 'til spring. Most is still a bit green, and it would dry out faster when split. So this latest turn of events is a bit of a bummer.

I guess I'll use this brief hiatus to achieve a little work inside. Again . . . it sucks getting old. Sometimes I still think and act like I'm in my twenties, then my body says 'oh no you fool, you can't do this anymore'...oh joy!

Wood chips in my bed...it's nice having a dog around—especially this one—but no matter how often I sweep the floor to keep wood chips out, Kiyo manages to tote a few into bed with him every night. I am constantly brushing the darned things out from between the sheets. And, when he is outside long enough to soak up some wet snow—we sleep in a wet bed. Never know what to expect with Kiyo as my bedmate.

We had fog up here today—ice fog—the kind that creates sparkling ice crystals suspended from every the tree limb and twig. This early morning fog is a first for me, for the mist usually hovers far below my cabin's lofty perch while I remain drenched in bright sunshine. But today I sit idly, gazing out from my glass-fronted observation site, savoring my morning coffee, totally engrossed with the spectacle of the sun's slow penetration through the dense cloud-like stuff below. Then with unexpected and startling suddenness, she broke through onto my mountaintop, shooting radiant beams into every nook and cranny, and transforming each ice-coated tree into dazzling glassy behemoths. As though in harmony a breeze stirred up from the South and the trees began to dance—their ice crystals tinkling like a heavenly choir, and flashing their icy sun-lit gems like the finest of diamonds. It was a kind of spiritual moment; absolutely beautiful. I sat transfixed at the cabin's front window, mesmerized by the trees as they dipped and swayed in the breeze, dancing, as if in a ball room, showing off their finery—and just for me. Later the sun melted the cloak of ice, the breeze waned, and the trees resumed their stately presence once again, perhaps in wait for the next round of ice fog.

These are the moments that ease my mind, cleanse me. I love it here; the beauty—the quite—bestow me with a peace I haven't felt in years. I never want to leave this place. Nothing can compare to the beauty of a forest in winter. I now fully understand Robert Frost's poem about the woods in winter.

"The woods are lovely, dark and deep.
But I have promises to keep,
and miles to go before I sleep . . ."
  —Robert Frost

The dogsled is working out great so far. It flipped over just once when I took the turn from Ernest's T's place to my just a little too sharp. But if I keep my wits about me it's doing an admirable job. I had planned to rig up and attach a set of outriggers to keep it from flipping, but now I believe it may not be necessary. I am toying with a better way to hook it up to the snowmobile. Right now just using a one inch strap attached from the snowmobiles' rear "bumper" to two eye hooks on the dog sled. It works fine going up hill, but the sled runs into the back of the snowmobile when traveling down hill, pushing the runners into the track. This could cause the runners to break off. So it's imperative to come up with a better solution. Oh well—it will give me something to work on while my wood chopping days have been curtailed.

The little generator I bought was hyped to run five-hours with a full load on it. I don't have near a full load on it, and its run for almost ten hours, and this for two days in a row. This is great! I can keep the solar batteries charged (when the sun's not shining), run my TV, and also keep my home phone charged. I bought a wireless home phone from AT&T a few weeks back. It's meant to be a booster for a home phone. It works great as long as I keep it charged, and it can hone in on a good signal. With this little convenience I won't have to rely on my cell phone—which is 'spotty' up here when signals are weak. Communication is pretty darn necessary when you live so far away from civilization.

As I mentioned earlier when spring arrives I'm planning to build a deck off the front of the cabin and wrap it around onto a roofed-over deck along the east wall. Probably stretch it out 8 feet to allow me the luxury of sitting outside in nice weather. If I roof it over I'll be able to enjoy watching the advance of thunder storms sweeping in from across the mountains. I enjoy a good thunder storm. My whole family is a little 'nuts' that way. I remember watching those storms roll in off the bay when we lived in Castine, Maine. My sister, mom and I would hunker down in front of one of the third floor bedroom windows and marvel at the wrath of the storms as they moved in and over us.

I've got the old 2x4's, full of nails, that Larry gifted me. He wasn't going to waste his time pulling them, but I will. Nothing like reclaimed lumber to get things going around here. Now I can begin to frame in the back wall near the roof, and do it right. The last owner incorrectly attached metal roofing to cover the top of the wall, with no insulation, or properly binding it in. I will frame it in and cover over the existing windows. Once the addition is in place those windows become useless. This modification should also keep a little more heat inside. Then I plan to frame in and insulate the big upper window for the same reasons. The only things left needing more insulation are around the rafters over the stove. That will obviously have to wait until spring as the stovepipe is to damn hot to be messing with.

24

February, and the 'Ole Man Settles In, Letting Loose the Wrath of the Mountain Gods Upon Us

February, with all the charm of an uninvited uncle—has been the worst month for me on my mountain. First it snowed *and snowed* ... dumping more than three feet of new snow at my place. Next, I was called upon to leave my utopian abode to deliver a Canadian load. Then, upon my return the motor in my old reliable pickup gave up—died—leaving me with no transportation. So, with my options suddenly few to none, I ended up under another load—this time to Iowa. When I got back from that run I discovered that both of Ernest T's pickups had broken down leaving Sherylee and their kids stranded up on the mountain. And me? I was stranded down below—off the mountain. It had snowed so much while I was gone, alternating with rainy ice-storms that the road had become un-traversable. I'd made a bad miscalculation. I had stupidly left my snowmobile at Ernest T's place near the top of the mountain. In my defense, I thought I'd only be gone a few days—never dreamed that my semi-retirement job would keep me on the road for such an extended period of time—time for winter to raise havoc with my best-laid plans.

You know the 'stuff' that trickles downhill? It would seem this adage kicked into high gear this month. Moe's elderly and ill mother died while I was away and she and Larry left hurriedly for California to attend her funeral. While they were gone their water pipes froze, burst, and flooded a good part of their home. No—February was definitely not a good month for anyone on this mountain.

When I did finally make it up the road to Ernest T's place my goal was to get my snowmobile and ride it up the final quarter-mile to my cabin. Instead I discovered that because it had been sitting so long, with less than half a tank of fuel, the resulting condensation had created a bad gas situation and it would not keep running for more than a minute or two. So, although so close to my cabin I could almost smell it, I could not get up to it. The remaining road between his place and mine was laden with deep punky, slushy, water-logged snow. It would be nearly impossible to get anything through that muck—a snowmobile would sink in, snowshoes might do it but—gee—there I go again—my pair are hanging on my cabin walls. I cringe when imagining the circus frenzy going on up there in my absence—hoards of darling little mice rampaging about in the bag of dog food I left unsecured.

Larry and Dawn arrived back from California and invited me to bunk at their place for the weekend. The food and climate are always grand and comfortable in their home so I put my frustrations on the back burner and enjoyed my time with them before heading back out on the road again. Yep!—on the road again! Might as well make some extra money so when I'm finally able to get back up to my mountain top I'll be in good financial shape to begin the work on my cabin. I can't wait! *Please* Spring hurry up! Although I'm reminded this has been one the area's milder winters, with far less snow than the norm, the inimitable circumstances of this February have been such as to prevent me from living the life I had anticipated; safe and secure, cozy and comfy in my cabin in the woods. Talk about frustration!

"Life is what happens to you while you're busy making other plans."
—John Lennon

On The Road Again
(thanks Willie)

Oh how the Fates have messed with my plans. Couldn't get to my cabin. Couldn't get to my stash of clothes, meds, dog food or any other of my belongings. Couldn't believe my own dumb bad luck. How stupid of me to allow for such a short-sighted blunder—setting in motion the chain of events keeping me away from my beloved Chez Walden. I could only imagine my lonely cabin hunkering down without me—withstanding the onslaughts of Winter. And now, Kiyo and I are once again navigating the byways, living in the truck. Damn! Lesson learned (how many of these will there be?). I won't let this situation sneak up on me another winter.

On the plus side—being away from my adored retreat has allowed me the space and time to consider—and reconsider—the many options I have planned for her.

I began by rethinking the well—and the root cellar. Earnest T paid around $10,000 for his well and it's 250 feet deep. I've discovered there is a 10-acre lot above mine where someone long ago dug a 500 foot deep well. No one seems to know who, or why—as no one lives up there. That well, deep as it is, only pumps one to two gallons per minute. Way too damn slow. At that rate, if I had a well dug, I would certainly have to install a cistern for water storage. So now I'm toying with the idea of a rain water collection system for my water needs; bathing, dishes and if I filter it, can maybe even use it for drinking. I have two water tanks harvested from a couple of travel trailers as well as one still inside Casa Del Fifth Wheel. Together these would total around a 300-gallon storage capacity. I also own three 55-gallon plastic drums and with a few more I could store enough rain water for all my needs, for immediate use and into the future. Now to figure out how to keep them from freezing during the winter.

Now: about that fridge and the few other items that need power. Since batteries can't be allowed to freeze, I am mulling over the prospect of digging a root cellar. I briefly considered burying the truck body for this purpose—situating it under the new addition—or I could simply bury it in the backyard, behind the cabin.

Next: I want the breaker box located in such a way that will not necessitate running any wires underground. I first considered placing it along a kitchen wall, but until I can run all the necessary wiring that location could impede my progress in hanging drywall—or attaching the much needed shelves. And my kitchen definitely needs shelving. It's overflowing with pots, pans, and dishes piled temporarily on top of the fridge. It is exceedingly frustrating not to be able to go forth with all these plans. Once I get back into my cabin I may just plow ahead with the wiring and hope I don't make a mistake. If I miscalculate it will be a real bitch to re-open the walls to make any changes—not to mention the additional costs.

> "Many a slip twix the cup and the lip."
> —William Shakespeare from *Hamlet*

Then there's the issue of getting an excavator up there to dig the holes. It would be costly. They charge by the hour, and as slow as these things move it would take three-hours to drive one up, then the cost of digging, then add to that the cost of the return trip down the mountain. I think it's out of my budget. But *I know a guy* with a small tractor, equipped with a backhoe attachment, and is willing to do my bidding on the mountain. However, the terrain around the cabin is rocky so I don't know how effective his machine would be. But, bottom line—it would take far too long to dig a hole large enough for a root cellar by hand, so a gutsy piece of equipment needs to be considered. I'm going to have to improvise and find simpler and more effective ways to achieve my dreams up there without it costing me a fortune. What would Henry David do?

It's an ill wind that . . . well—you know the rest.

While traversing about the countryside I got a phone call from my Mom and sister. They'd been out 'antiquing'—doing something they thoroughly enjoy—traipsing through the junk shops, second-hand stores, and antique emporiums in their Florida neighborhood. They had just stumbled upon a charming vintage kitchen range with amazing eye-appeal. This classic gem flaunted four gas-fired stove-top burners, plus a deep fire pit for burning wood and/or coal. She was encased in a pale green coat of enamel. They instantly forwarded a picture to me and quoted a price tag I couldn't refuse. I could already visualize her—proud and formidable—enhancing my kitchen. "Would the owner hold it 'til I could get there?" The answer was "Yes."

I knew that within the next few months I would be hauling a piece of equipment to mid-Florida. The shop owner slapped a "sold" sign on her and delighted in telling everybody that she was destined for a mountaintop in Idaho. It was three months before I finally got to meet this lady and pick her up. When I say 'pick up' I don't want to infer that she made it easy for me. This lady had substance. I ended up hiring four men and a pickup truck to load her, transport her to my rig, then reload her onto my flatbed. I'm guessing she weighed near 500 pounds.

When I get her back to Idaho I will leave her in the talented hands of a *guy a know* who will weld on a proper fitting, capable of connecting her backside to my propane setup. Sadly "Ancient Agatha" will be forced into her second—and probably last—retirement. Her repairs and reconditioning issues were proving to be far too extensive and costly. This 'new' interloper will be far superior both in efficiency and beauty.

My New Charmer Begins Her Journey to Idaho.

A Reprieve. And With the Woman Who's Stealin' My Heart.

While I was on the road Tracy was planning our fourth date: a 10-day vacation to the Dominican Republic. It was a gift for my 53rd birthday (April 5th) and slated for the end of March. Our traveling companions would include her sister and brother-in-law. I was ecstatic! I had never been to the islands before. It would be both therapeutic and romantic. What a gal! While smiling ear to ear as I jockeyed my rig down the road it occurred to me that I would need my summer clothes wardrobe which, of course, was on top of the mountain. With the bounty offer by the local Goodwill Shops and the generosity of her Dad (he and I are the same size) I managed to pull together an acceptable holiday wardrobe before departure day.

I still had some driving to do, and some loads to deliver before I could even think about dipping my toes in the warm blue waters of the tropics. But the mere notion of it warmed me—beaconing me like a moth to a flame. Tracy and I texted hourly—Facebooked daily. Phone calls were out of the question. The price of calls in and out of Canada was a luxury only for the independently wealthy. Tropical Islands—here I come!

I passed the next few weeks daydreaming, and when I couldn't sleep, I dreamed of spring and the fun I'd have tickin' things off the list of completed projects at Chez Walden. The list grows nightly.

>   Build porch and deck
>   Install a new and more efficient roof on cabin
>   Shop for a new wood-burning stove
>   Build my new addition
>   Come up with an effective water storage system
>   Buy or build a composting toilet
>   Procure bigger and better batteries
>   Buy and install more solar panels
>   Plan for, and create, a wind turbine
>   Build a hearth for the primary stove from the abundant supply of stones scattered about the property
>   Install a real shower
>   Re-insulate the main cabin
>   Sheet rock the kitchen and main cabin walls
>   Get all wiring done, both 12-volt and 110
>   Find a better way to traverse the mountain in winter

I've decided to take the month of June off from trucking to be able to start checking off some of those items. I'm anxious to frame in a porch on the east side. And while the roof is off I plan to tie in the rafters from the porch into the main roof. I also think I'll extent the porch around to the cabin's front creating a great 'sitting' deck. It will be a pretty addition, plus making it easier to keep snow and dirt from being tracked inside the cabin. It will afford me a great vantage spot to sit and enjoy the view whilst I sip my coffee (or wine if Tracy's here.) My Mom's informed me she expects a rocking chair sitting there in wait for her when she visits.

25

It was the beginning of March before I made it back to St. Maries and attempted another stab at climbing my mountain. Not to be. The road up to my cabin was two feet deep in rutted untraversable packed snow. Ernest T hadn't been able to drag the road while his trucks were in for repairs, and during that period the snow had packed hard, so when he finally did attempt to drag it, it was a disaster. The wheels of his truck broke through the heavily crusted snow creating two deep channels. His truck body sits higher than mine—giving him an elevated ground clearance. My pickup sits lower—so when I tried following in his tracks my truck undercarriage got hung up on the ruts, and I was unable to move. My snowmobile—which might have gotten me up to Chez Walden was still languishing up the mountain on his doorstep. My cabin might as well have been on the moon.

Now Comes the Good Part

Nick had managed to find me a load heading to Calgary the week before we were scheduled to fly out to our tropic paradise. A soon as it was safely off-loaded I pointed the rig toward Edmonton and Tracy's cozy condo. We spent a great week together before our flight. This was to be the test of our relationship—the longest period of time we would be together. Would we still like each other at the other end? Time will tell.

Then the flight from weather-ridiculous to weather-sublime. Into the heat! You don't realize just how cold you've been until you land in the Dominican Republic. Once off the plane, and out of the terminal it hits you like a brick wall—and Damn did it feel good! I can handle eight days of this, and paradise too.

We spent days exploring and sightseeing, dining on epicurean delights, and sipping the best rums the Island had to offer—and the rum produced here is world-famous. We met charming people—our wait staff—the villagers—the cab drivers. We fell in love with it all—and each other. One of our most memorable excursions took us to a waterfall that boasts 27 separate mini-falls—twelve of which you can slide down on your butt, just like a carnival waterslide. Talk about fun! Then we rode a Zipline for six-miles, ogling the magnificence scenery below us. We sailed on a catamaran and snorkeled in the deep blue sea. We rode horseback and toured the city with a super congenial cab driver. I ticked more things off my 'bucket list' in a short space of time than I ever thought possible. It was all splendid fun. We met some great people who invited us into their homes and fed us the most amazing food. And of course there's the beach. We swam, sunbathed and buried each other in sand.

All to soon it was time to go. We promised each other we would return again next year. We packed our summer garb, safely stowed away our memories, and boarded the plane back to 'Ole Man Winter.

Fourth date—fourteen days together—and we still like each other.

My Love and I.

Snorkeling in the
Deep Blue Sea.

> "There is only one path to Heaven. On Earth, we call it Love."
> —Henry David Thoreau

Back to the Real World

April was pretty much a duplicate of March. The snow was two to three feet deep on the mountain and getting up to the cabin was not going to happen. If someone invented a word beyond "frustrated" I want access to it for that would express my feelings exactly. But since there was nothing I could do about it, but wait out the winter's hangover, I continued hauling freight for Nick.

If Winter Comes Can Spring Be Far Behind?

Spring has finally come to Northern Idaho. Fields are drying out. Farmers are beginning to plow. Grass is turning green, and flowers are blooming everywhere. Except on the mountain. Up there two feet of snow still has a stubborn hold on my driveway. And the stuff stills clings obstinately to the road between Ernest T's drive and mine. Needless to say, I can't even consider navigating my pickup up that last quarter-mile.

It would be the second week of May before I actually got body and soul up to Chez Walden and only then because Larry hauled me and Kiyo up there on his four wheeler. It would be another two weeks before I was able to negotiate my own pickup to Ernest T's place—and hike up the last few hundred feet (that's up hill—an eleven% grade—for one quarter mile—whine, whine, whine). It would be another week before I could finally swing my pickup into my own driveway.

But now the snow was melting away quickly, though 18-inches of the stuff still clung obstinately on and about the cabin. But like watching a slow-motion video, I could witness its' demise at it sluggishly melted away—revealing what lay beneath—undone chores. By the end of my first weekend back on the top—it had all disappeared. Yeah Spring!

"On the morning of many a first spring day… the woods were bathed in so pure and bright a light as would have waked the dead. There needs no stronger proof of immortality."
—Henry David Thoreau

What to Do First?

The first thing I did when I arrived was to open all the windows, and air the place out. Then begin a mouse-clean-up. In my absence they'd moved in, and had one hell-of-a-time hosting back-to-back parties for all their buddies. A mice eviction notice will be my next project. A cat would do nicely but I will not chance one becoming coyote bait. I'll have to find a way to convince them to leave. I've heard that peppermint can do the job.

As I began policing and cleaning up around the perimeters of the cabin I discovered a number of items I thought I'd lost. But apparently they were only wintering it out under the snow. My wood pile collapsed, and the snow-melt revealed two pickup loads of logs still patiently waiting to be split. So guess I'll soon resume my wood-splitting chores. The wood pile needs to be moved anyway, to make it more accessible—and dry—in bad weather. Next I hope to jockey the truck body closer to the cabin, turning it every so slightly so its' door faces toward the cabin. Work—work—work! But, I'm reminded—this is how I managed to peal off those forty pounds in short order.

"If one advances confidently in the direction of his dreams, and endeavors to live the life which he has imagined, he will meet with success unexpected in common hours."
—Henry David Thoreau

Early one morning, bolstered and buoyed by a rasher of bacon, a few sunny-side-up eggs, and several cups of strong, hot coffee, with Kiyo bouncing along at my heels, I hiked over to the lot abutting mine. It faces south with a magnificent view of the St. Joe River. Even with the decaying mush of punky snow and ice still stubbornly clinging to its pathway, it was a pleasant little jaunt. Now with weather warming up I hope to take more hikes—out, about, and around "my" mountain. What a way to start the day!

> "An early-morning walk is a blessing for the whole day."
> —Henry David Thoreau

The peace up here is almost palpable and having been away for so long I appreciate it all the more. Now I can once again relax—unwind and be as one with the world. I'm not a religious man, but if heaven exists, I would want it to resemble this mountaintop utopia. After all I have been through: the stress of military service; the pressure of driving a rig; that ugly divorce; this is my fortress—my strength—my recharging station. A huge benefit of this Eden is that I experience less pain, and therefore have been able to reduce the amount of medication needed. I believe the nerve disease is healing itself, and though I will never be totally free of the muscle disease, I believe it's lessened its gripe on me.

> "Every people have gods to suit their circumstances."
> —Henry David Thoreau

There don't appear to be any hardwood trees up here. It's all fir. I hope to plant a few maples later to give my ten acres a splash of color in the fall. I know it may sound silly—planting trees in a forest—but when one grows up in New England, surrounded by maples, and oaks, and other hard wood trees, one misses the fall colors. And so I will plant trees that will give me a sense of my old home...and bring a dash of autumn brilliance into this already magnificent mountaintop.

Just a note: There's been a redheaded woodpecker hovering about my cabin these past two mornings and he's been making a hell-of-a racket, searching for 'woodpecker-gold' in a cedar tree just outside my front window. I grabbed a picture of him before he flew off. Glad I did, for he hasn't come back. Either he's camera-shy or there simply weren't enough good bugs to be had in my cedar.

Visiting Woodpecker.

Logging trucks are starting to be of concern now as they begin their annual operations in the areas near my end of my road. When I drove down into town today I couldn't help but notice there were trees cut and stacked on either side of the road. At one hairpin turn a large tree top was sprawled across the road and I had to drag it off to the side before I could drive any further. A potential problem of their activity up here is the possibility of them closing off road. That would be a huge issue for those of us who live on this mountain. Of even greater concern, the drivers of these logging trucks don't expect to encounter other drivers on these roads and they tend to drive too fast. Then too, there are a number of blind corners that pose a hazard for anyone traversing either up or down—and there's no place for vehicles to pass on this road. If I was to encounter a truck either way, one of us would have to back up. Since I'm the smaller guy—I believe the adage "size-matters" would apply in this standoff, and I'd be the backer-upper! Fortunately, once I'm up here I don't have to drive down that road too often. When I do I'm overly cautious—I certainly don't want a head on confrontation with a logging truck.

> "If a man walks in the woods for love of them half of each day, he is in danger of being regarded as a loafer. But if he spends his days as a speculator, shearing off those woods and making the earth bald before her time, he is deemed an industrious and enterprising citizen."
> —Henry David Thoreau

26

> "You only need sit still long enough in some attractive spot in the woods that all its inhabitants may exhibit themselves to you by turns."
> —Henry David Thoreau

The young critters are out and about now. A few nights ago while heading up the mountain, I spooked a cow moose and her calf. The next morning as I drove down I came across a deer and her fawn. She showed no fear—just stood there quietly—watching me as her fawn wandered about nearby—then together they strode off into the woods. These aren't the only neighbors I've encountered. The tree in front of my place seems a favorite perch of two young redheaded woodpeckers. They've have been showing up a few times a day, squabbling over coveted epicurean creepy-crawlies that inhabit the bark. Rabbits too, have sat right outside my door and seem to be everywhere. For fun and entertainment I leave tidbits on the deck for any critters that might come along. It pleases me to watch the antics of my four-footed neighbors. They seem to sense I will not harm them, and linger nearby as though I am their protector. Kiyo doesn't seem too happy about the arrangement, but he leaves them alone.

A guy I know asked me if I had cedar trees around my place and told me cedars like shallow water as their roots don't go deep. If this was the case I could "develop" a spring and maybe not have to punch a well at all. Now I have never heard of this technique, but he claims that all I have to do is look for a draw nearby where water would be channeled during spring runoff, and where the snow melts off first, then dig down until I hit water (he says not far—8 to 10 feet). I don't know how true this might be but I might just poke around and see what I find.

I've begun gathering up rocks around my place with the goal of using these rustic little gems to build a few things; starting with a stone hearth and stone wall under and behind the wood stove as well as the kitchen range. This will allow me to get rid of the ugly metal sheathing on the wall, greatly enhancing the look of the place, plus adding a safety factor. I also want to build a stone planter for the front porch-to-be though I'm not sure what type of vegetation it will hold. I do believe it will add a nice touch and give a more finished look to the outside.

A Reunion is Planned

During the months of exile from Chez Walden a plan began to formulate between my former Navy buddies and I. We have always kept in touch through a variety of means: email, Facebook, via phone, and the occasional brief get-together. The vision of a reunion has often been the topic of our conversations. But where to hold it—and when? Well, Damn! How about on my mountaintop? Walla! The idea not only takes hold but the plans assure it will become a reality. Word went out to everybody and a an approximate date was set—some weekend in June. "Can I bring the wife?" " Can I bring the kids?" "Can we target-shoot up there?" Tents, sleeping bags, food, cookers, and guns became the hot topics as plans began to fall into place. Even my gal Tracy got into the act making plans to fly down for the reunion.

I had to work fast. I wanted to get the new porch and deck built, and maybe even get it roofed-over before Tracy's arrival. It would be such fun to lounge outside on a completed deck for morning coffee. Plus it would enhance the heck out of the cabin and impress my Navy buddies when they descend upon the place.

You can get pissed off at what life throws at you or you can laugh about it, and forge ahead—doing the best you can. This was June and my plan was to take the month off, tear off the roof, install OSB Plywood—then reroof the whole business, and build the deck. Moreover, I desperately wanted to start the new addition. At the very least I hoped to get it dried in before winter and snow accumulations prevent me from hauling material all the way up to my cabin. Dried in generally means that the house is protected from the weather (dry in = dry inside).

Roofing felt is on, exterior sheathing has been installed, exterior doors are hung, and windows are installed. With all needed supplies I can finish off the inside while 'ole Man Winter throws his weight around outside.

This was not to be. On June 2nd I drove into town and bought a whole unit of 2x6x8's of lumber (a unit consists of about 180 plus boards). This is a heavy load for my old pickup, but I felt she could handle it with relative ease. However, as I headed up the mountain road I realized the old girl was getting a little hot, not overheating, but close. I decided to pull into Earnest T's place and let her cool down a bit before making the last ¼ mile up to my place. As I sat enjoying a coffee with Sherylee, her son came dashing in yelling that my truck was smoking. I ran outside and sure enough—she was. This was not the kind of smoke that indicates an overheated motor, but the kind that spells fire! I quickly raced to her, opened the hood and with a fire extinguisher in hand quickly snuffed out the flames. Once the dust and smoke had settled I perused the damage and determined the fire had burned up the distributer, the spark plug wires, and the ignition coil. Additionally it melted away the coverings on some essential wiring but hadn't melted the wires themselves. So, here I was with a truck load of lumber, a quarter-mile from my place, and I can't move.

The next week was split between moving my load of lumber up—bit by bit—with the help of Sherylee and her truck, and working on repairing the fried innards of my pickup. By the end of the week, with all new parts installed the damn thing still wouldn't start. Well lucky for me *I know a guy*! A guy with a wreaker! And a shop at his wreaking yard. With this connection I got the old girl back in less than a week, and running good as new. The cause of the fire? It seems the oil in the ignition coil had sprung a leak, bathing an already hot motor with hot oil and setting it ablaze. Not a real big deal. The fire could have left me without a truck at all. But nevertheless, it raised havoc with my plans.

The Deck Takes Shape

I have a my deck finished. All that's needed now is to water-seal it. The porch along the cabin's front is also coming along nicely, though I still need to hang the porch rafters. Before that can be done I've got to remove the metal roofing. The last owner simply laid the metal roofing over the rafters. Not a smart piece of construction. I plan to take it off, lay down OSB plywood, then tarpaper over all before covering all with new metal roofing, greatly enhancing the view from outer-space as the current roofing is three different shades of green. This procedure will also right the many of the wrongs done by the last owner and provide me with a snug, air-tight abode prior to the frigid blasts of 'ole Man Winter's wrath. As I move forward with the remodeling I further discovered 2x4" bats of insulation loosely stuck in between 2x6" stud openings, leaving 2-inch unprotected gaps throughout. And much of this doesn't even extend fully to the tops or bottoms between the studs. This explains why it was so damn cold in here last winter. I've no choice but to replace all the insulation, and install a vapor barrier (Plastic sheeting affixed between the interior wall and the insulation thus preventing moisture from seeping in and encouraging mold to grow). This is crucial to the cabin's health and wellbeing. Additionally, there are no heel plates in-between the rafters, allowing for all manner of wind, weather, snow and rain to find its way inside. Surprisingly—I don't mind righting all these pass transgressions. It kind of relaxes me after a long week of haulin' freight.

Kitchen Kapers

Finally I got to tackle the kitchen wiring and set it up for both 110 and 12 volts. Among other things this will make it easier to sell the place—should I ever decide to sell it. But for now I can hang the sheetrock and paint proper walls. Haven't decided on a color yet—maybe a light green. That would compliment the "new" old beauty I trucked back from Florida. The old cast stove I lugged up here months ago, Ancient Agatha, was proving impossible to find parts for. My "new" beauty should prove far more versatile and efficient. So, with a little help from my friends I loaded the Ancient darlin' into the back of my pickup, toted her back down the mountain, and sold her for scrap. (Sniff.) The old gas range, scavenged from Casa Del Fifth Wheel, I put in storage—just in case I ever should need it.

Ma—the front deck is finished now and artfully tied to the side porch. I've only to haul a rocking chair up here—plant it front and center—and I'm ready for your visit. You're gonna love it!

We set a final date for the Navy reunion—the weekend of June 23rd and 24th.

Deck – Step 1.

Deck – Step 2.

Deck – Step 3.

27

The Path (Revisited)

The Path
(Revisited)
by
Benjamin M Scribner, written during second enlistment, circa 1988

I ask fate "Why?
What made my soul be chosen?"
But fate shall never answer.
I can feel them now...
The souls like mine,
Responding once more
To that far off trumpet's call.
To arms! To arms!
We shall beat our plowshares into swords,
And begin our grisly work (how we loath the task!).
When the deed is done
In years to come
For those of us left standing
We shall sit with our kith and kin
And raise a toast
To those brave souls left upon the field,
As they have done for us.

"Nothing makes the earth seem so spacious as to have friends at a distance; they make the latitudes and the longitudes."
—Henry David Thoreau

MIUWU 102
(Mobile Inshore Undersea Warfare Unit)

As I have stated emphatically several times throughout this tale, I served in the Navy and I'm damn proud of it!

Jan. 5 1942 Rear Admiral Ben Moreell as chief of the U.S. Navy's Bureau of Yards and Docks and of the Civil Engineer Corps gained the authority from the Bureau of Navigation to recruit men from the construction trades for three battalions for Navel Construction Battalions. A Seabee is a member of the United States Navy Construction Battalion (CB). The word "Seabee" comes from initials "CB." The Seabees have a history of building bases, bulldozing and paving thousands of miles of roadway and airstrips, and accomplishing a myriad of other construction projects in a wide variety of military theaters dating back to World War II.

Seabee's Motto: "We Build—We Fight." (Referenced from United States Seabees Museum and Memorial Park, Naval History and Heritage Command.)

When most people hear "Navy" they think "open sea." In my first enlisted incarnation I *was* on the open sea. I held the rank of 2nd class Petty Officer and my rate was TMT. I maintained the MK 46 torpedo for almost 10 years until my enlistment was up in 1988. Then came September 11th propelling me to the nearest recruiter's office and re-enlistment. This time, because of my truck driving experience, I was brought in as an equipment operator, or a Seabee. As a reservist I spent nearly a year sitting in a classroom for every drill weekend. I was ready to toss in the towel. The unit I was attached to had no equipment to operate and I was bored and disenchanted. Ripe for a change—I found it right under my nose—on the same drill compound I was already assigned to. At the rear of the compound sat two enormous buildings housing a huge supply of big equipment to play with. I hot-footed it over to ask if they needed any help. Turns out they did, and I was soon transferred to the MIUWU 102. Now at that time there were no active duty MIUW units in the Navy so the men in the reserve units trained every drill weekend as if we were an active unit. This suited me just fine and aside from working in my chosen element I'm happy to relate that I connected with some awesome men, many who became life-long friends. As time marched forward I was thrilled to discover this unit I'd been lucky enough to become attached to had set the benchmark for all other units in Uncle Sam's Navy. These sailors weren't just marking time until their enlistment was up, these guys *wanted* to be there, and many had earned multiple awards for their hard work. And before I left the unit I too had earned a few medals for my contributions. I had found a home!

A MIUWU's job is to guard a harbor from intruders on, or under, the water. We had many assets at our disposal: thermal imaging cameras, sonar buoys, and 'eyes on' (consists of sitting on a gun mount looking out at the vast expanse of ocean).

One year after I was assigned there we were deployed to South Korea for a two-week's training program. Before we were through we had impressed our Korean counterparts, and kicked ass in the process.

I guess I should back up here a minute in this narration to explain why this chapter is so important to my tale. I'm relating the friendships made during my Navy years, the characters of the men I served with, and the life-long bonds that were forged, for they will reappear in the chapter following. These men, their steel, their moral fiber, influenced my life for the better—then and now.

My first drill weekend with this unit was a four-day drill with a major inspection of the unit's readiness. One of the first people I had any contact with that first day was GM1 Dave Stern. With appropriate degree of authority he instructed me that later that night I was to 'gain access' the compound. As promised—when night arrived he grabbed me, 'armed' me with a coke bottle wrapped in a wrist-watch, and told me to attempt to 'infiltrate the compound.' If this was not possible then I was to threaten the guards with my 'bomb' and see how far things went.

Here are some useful acronyms:

GM—Gunners mate
GM 1—Gunners mate first class
GMC—Gunners mate Chief
OSCS—Operations specialist Senior Chief
OS 1—Operations specialist first class
EO 2—Equipment operator second class
ET 1—Electronics Technician first class
TMT—Torpedo Man's Mate Tech
PTSD—Post Traumatic Stress Disorder

Well, I participated in this charade for almost a half hour before a guard stationed at the entrance to the compound 'shot' me. In the months following that little melodrama Dave and I became great friends and whiled away many an hour while standing watch in South Korea. I'll never know if my participation in 'infiltrating the base' was a legitimate training exercise or an exercise spun from his devious sense of humor. He's a damn funny guy and even all these years later he swears that someday he will cause liquid will shoot out my nose in response to one of his outlandish jokes. He slyly times his comic punches to coincide with me gulping a huge drink of some sort. (hasn't happened yet Dave).

While in South Korea I had the misfortune of drawing the bunk right above him. Misfortunate because Dave ate Kimchi (a popular Korean dish best described as a spicy, slightly sweet, pickled or fermented cabbage) three times a day. After two weeks I put in a requisition for a gas mask so I could breath at night.

Another remarkable guy I met during that period was GM1 John Richter. His job was with the weapons department. He took the job seriously but all the while retained a sense of humor. The man was a hard task master but he would never ask anyone to do something he wouldn't do himself. While working under John's command I became a line coach at the weapons range. (A line coach walks the line behind the shooters watching for any kind of trouble they might be having with their weapons). John was the RSO (Range Safety Officer), and a damn good one. He displayed the patience of Job with his new inexperienced recruits, working tirelessly to bring out the best in each one. I learned a lot about leadership and human-kindness from him. I respect him still for his leadership style.

GM1 Mark Bickham was another one of those guys who influenced my world and became a good buddy and life-long friend. He was our ammo guy—not an easy job in the Navy. Mark's job was to keep track of every single bullet we used, and how many rounds we expended, and what we still had on hand. One screw-up and he could wind up in deep do-do. I'm surprised he's still on this side of the turf. With the stresses of his job I was sure he would drop dead of a heart attract.

OS1 Rick Smawley was another member of my watch section. His job was in the command center, or MOC as it was called over there, while my job was on a gun mount. Smawley was no doubt the most organized guy I know, and probably the genius of our company. His job required extensive record keeping. I never saw him without his clipboard on which he was constantly scribbling. (Were you writing about me?)

ET1 Earl Johnson was one of a handful of "rip to fills" (see below) that stayed with the unit long after we came home. He was a standout in many ways—and not just because of his 6'10" frame. A quiet guy—but when he spoke—you listened. He must be commended for withstanding continuous assaults upon his name. "Big Johnson" jokes flew fast and furious. (Ladies, if you don't understand this joke ask your closest male friend.) He'd heard them all since school days so was pretty immune and took them in stride. Because he wasn't in my watch section our contact was a bit scanty. We often passed "like ships in the night," he coming off duty, me going on. But like all the others we stayed in touch long after returning to stateside.

I'll never forget OSC Sean Barley. Sean was the kind of Chief that took no shit from anyone, officer or enlisted. But he also stood up for his people. If you were in the right, he would back you up 100%, but God help you if you were wrong. In my one memorable run-in with him, his particular style of leadership became apparent to me while we served together in the Persian Gulf (Kuwait). In the 'old' Navy, that I had come from, men were not allowed to wear bracelets of any kind.

Times have changed and in this 'new' Navy enlisted men are allowed to wear them—as long as they're not big and gaudy, or those ugly rubber things that tote messages. I have worn a silver bracelet for years—since I got out of active duty—and I continued to do so. Sean confronted me one day stating that my bracelet was not acceptable. I told him it was, and he challenged me to prove it. So I looked up the Navy regulations regarding bracelets, made a copy, and presented it to him. He smiled, admitted he knew it all along. He just wanted to see if I would make the effort to research and stand my ground. "Good job" was his reply with a slight twinkle in his eye. High praise from a man of his caliber and a prime demonstration of his unique leadership style. He wanted the men under his command to question—research—and prove him right or wrong—and then to stand by their convictions. He added another layer to my understanding of good leadership. A good man. Another who will have my respect for life.

There are many others of those who served with me I could mention here, but these are the ones that have been the most influential in my life, and have stayed in contact with me since.

Things soon got serious and orders arrived for our deployment. When a unit deploys and there aren't enough live bodies to fill all the requirements of it's mission, the Navy does what it calls 'rip to fill'—which simply stated means grabbing enlisted people from all over the country and stuffing them into the understaffed unit. Overnight we seemed to tripled in size. The downside of this procedure is that some of these enlisted men didn't want to be there, and consequently did the least amount of work necessary to get by—and then get out. Others grabbed at the chance, ran with it, and stayed with the unit even after we came home.

Our unit was then sent to San Diego for three months of training. These months were designed to mold us together as a functioning unit and, if necessary, a strong and highly functioning *fighting* unit. Then off we went to the Kuwait and the Persian Gulf.

Unfortunately near the end of our deployment in Gulf, while I was cross-rating, the ugly symptoms of a here-to-for unknown physical condition forced my return to the States, and into early retirement.

Fortunately all these fellow comrades, who became so influential in my life, have stayed in contact with me all these years since. Now comes talk of a reunion. What better place than on my mountaintop? All agree.

"Two sturdy oaks I mean, which side by side,
Withstand the winter's storm,
And spite of wind and tide,
Grow up the meadow's pride,
For both are strong
Above they barely touch, but undermined
Down to their deepest source,
Admiring you shall find
Their roots are intertwined
Insep'rably."
  —Henry David Thoreau

28

The Reunion

> "The language of Friendship is not words, but meanings.
> It is an intelligence above language."
> —Henry David Thoreau

My Buddies. My Brothers. The men and women from MIUWU—Mobile Inshore Undersea Warfare Unit. As plans marched forward for the anticipated reunion on my mountaintop, and the date was set, we burned up the airways with chatter; 'who's coming'—'who's been deployed'—'who's bringing a wife'—'who's bringing kids'—'who can't come this year but will next'—'who's bringing booze'—'who's bringing the beans and the beef'—'who's bringing the grill'—'who's bringing firearms.' The excitement grew, and everyone began gathering their camping gear, and stocking in enough water and food for an adventurous and glorious weekend high above the clouds. Unfortunately some wouldn't be able to attend. A few of them had been deployed—or were about to be. Some lived too far away. Others had previous obligations. But a goodly number were able to come—and did!

GMC (ret.) Dave Stern was the first up the mountain with his wife, and he was dragging behind his car the largest grill I'd ever seen. Boy did that come in handy! We made him head-chef for the weekend. They also trucked in enough food to feed a small army—as did the every other guy that followed.

ET1 (ret.) Earl Johnson was the next up, and once he arrived darkness was beginning to creep over the mountain, so we soon called it a night, and settled down for the evening.

The first up the mountain next day was OSCS (ret.) Sean Barley. He took one look around the place and said, "Wow! This is a PTSD'ers Heaven!" (Post Traumatic Stress Disorder). "Damn right!" I retorted. "It's away from the noise, the rat race, and crazy world below. A stressed fellow can de-stress up here, and flood his soul with peace and tranquility."

OSC (ret.) Rick Smawley was next up and though he couldn't stay the whole weekend, he had a great time while he was here and added a lot to the merriment of the gathering. While all others brought with them, what I'd term "significant" weaponry, Rick showed up with a *Star Trek Phaser*. He is a "Trekkie" after all (aren't most geniuses?) and had that ingenious little toy been real we could have had one heck-of-time.

GM1 (ret.) Mark Bickham showed up next, and later that evening GMC (ret) John Richter showed up with his whole family—wife and four kids. A whole family! That added another layer to our reunion and a great deal more interest.

That evening the night air was filled with the tantalizing aromas of the BBQ, and the primal lure of a flickering bonfire. We talked, we laughed, we reminisced, we told outrageous tales on each other, even shed a tear or two at some of the rememberings. No one got to bed before midnight. Some bedded down in tents they'd brought, some in the backs of their station wagons, and a few simply camped out under the stars.

My gal Tracy had flown down from Alberta to meet my buddies and totally enjoy the weekend of comradeship. The guys loved her, treating her to their caustic wit—just as though they'd known her forever. She gave back as good as she got.

The next day the flood gates of testosterone opened wide, inundating my piece of the mountaintop with an energy and drive never before seen in these parts. We guys spent the day showing off—and shooting off—our various and sundry collection of weaponry. The air became heavy with the scent of gun powder, musky-manliness, with just a pinch of military might.

"We cannot but pity the boy who has never fired a gun."
—Henry David Thoreau

While the guys were all focused on flexing their military might, attempting to destroy every clay disc in their reserve, the gals lounged happily up at the cabin, and chatted about whatever gals chat about.

A couple of them already knew each other and they all quickly banded together—laughed a lot—emptied a couple of wine bottles—laughed some more—and appeared to be enjoying the day with as much gusto as we were. (Was it because of their Navy affiliations?—the rarified atmosphere of the mountaintop?—the wine?—or the age-old 'them vs. us?' We'll never know.) At any rate they hit it off and had a great time. Earlier in the day John's wife and kids hiked up to the acreage above mine to witness the spectacular views offered from the south side of the mountain.

All four kids of John's participated in the target practice throughout the day. Each of them have been extensively trained in the proper handling of firearms, but nevertheless we all kept a watchful eye on them. His sixteen-year-old daughter regularly participates in competitive shooting meets, and managed to upstage her dad—much to the delight of the rest of us. While laying prone on a blanket with her .22 rifle (a weapon so quiet that with our protective hearing plugs we could not hear it when fired), she watched her dad fire away at one of the clay targets. He fired three rounds—and missed each time. As he walked away shaking his head his daughter took aim at the target he had missed—and it exploded! If I'd only had a video camera to freeze that moment in time. I could have harassed John with it for years. His retort? He claimed his bullets were too slow.

The food was never-ending and the grill ran non-stop. There were beans and hot dogs, hamburgers, steaks, and salads, breads, rolls, and outrageously decedent desserts. Dave trucked up a huge rack of ribs, as had Tracy and I. He started slow cooking them early in the day and by the time we were ready to eat the meat nearly melted off the bones. We also had the fixins' for a toothsome pasta salad, and to that add ears of buttered corn-on-the-cob, grilled to perfection. We ate and drank ourselves silly.

The kids obviously reveled in camping out and playing with their parents on top of a mountain.

By Sunday night it was over. Sadly everyone trekked down my mountain to resume their daily nine-to-five. I felt each had left a small piece of their heart behind and each was just a bit envious of my life up here above the clouds. Who wouldn't be?

Now the word is out, and I'm hearing from those that weren't able to attend how sorry they are not to have been here. They won't make that mistake again. Next year. Next year! Is the united chant. Yes . . . we'll do it again next year, and I've no doubt the number will double. Those that were deployed will be back, and ready for some R&R. Those that had 'previous obligations' will clear their calendar. Those that live too far away will make advance plans.

I must admit—I was tuckered out by weekend's end—as was Tracy. We slept away most of Monday and recovered nicely. I'm back up-and-running now and looking forward to the next reunion. By this time next year I should have all the cabin's extensions and improvements completed—or at least near-completion. Meanwhile, I'll begin keeping my eye out for a large grill to add to my growing 'toy collection' up here. Maybe not as big as the one Dave pulled up the mountain, but close.

St. Crispin's Day Speech of Shakespeare's King Henry V. 1598:

This story shall the good man teach his son;

And Crispin Crispian shall ne'er go by,

From this day to the ending of the world,

But we in it shall be remember'd;

We few, we happy few, we band of brothers;

For he to-day that sheds his blood with me

Shall be my brother; be he ne'er so vile,

This day shall gentle his condition:

And gentlemen in England now a-bed

Shall think themselves accursed they were not here,

And hold their manhoods cheap whiles any speaks

That fought with us upon Saint Crispin's day.

Testosterone Flooded the Mountain.

Target Practicing.

The Food Just Kept on Coming.

29

Can't Seem to Get That Trucking Behind Me

It's been a frustrating year since I purchased my piece of Utopia last Fall. I had so many great plans and dreams for living in comfort—off-the-grid, adding an ell onto the cabin's southern end, finishing off the kitchen, building decks and porches, and new roofs, and so many other projects that I've mapped out, and related in this accounting. However, life gets in the way and of necessity I've spent more time away from Chez Walden then I had hoped—or planned for. So many of these projects still remain unfinished and wait to be accomplished. The beat goes on.

My friend, and boss Nick, and I have been shuttling freight around the countryside for over 19 years. He calls the shots and his wife keeps the books, and I usually just go where he sends me. A good team. He stood by me during my one-year stint in Kuwait—and again for the year of rehabilitation that followed. He acted as buffer and supported during the ugly months of my divorce wrangling. He always had a job for me—and I respect that kind of loyalty. Now, since April, he has lost four trucks due to various causes and complications, and his small company has grown smaller still. The first truck he lost was to a wreck. The driver, a good friend of mine, rolled his truck, totaling it. Luckily he walked away from it in one piece, but was pretty banged up. He's in his 60s and decided he'd had enough—time to leave the trucking business to the youngsters coming through the pipeline. Nick's second truck was retired because its driver, in his 70s, was dealing with failing eyesight. A wise move to retire when you can not longer read the road signs. Truck #3 was lost because the young driver had a wife who didn't want him away for extended periods, and decided it was beneficial to his marriage that he pursue another line of work. Truck #4 was lost because that driver and his wife chose to move back to their home state of Alabama.

So because I have been with Nick since he started his company, and he's my friend, I have agreed to do what I can to help out. I agreed to take local loads *only* "unless you are in a real bind." Suddenly I'm under loads going to Texas and Georgia. I didn't know they were local! But it happened. I can't leave a good friend in a bind, so I do what I can. So now those improvements to the cabin will simply have to wait. What I don't get finished this summer, I will finish in the Fall...or next summer. No hurry. (Sob.) The up-side of this (thank god for up-sides) means money is piling up in my savings account. When I finally get to perform all the miracle solutions to the Chez, I'll have all the funds needed to do them and (hopefully) do them right the first time.

> "Make the most of your regrets;
> never smother your sorrow,
> but tend and cherish it till it comes to have
> a separate and integral interest.
> To regret deeply is to live afresh."
> —Henry David Thoreau

I've Always Loved a Good Storm.

First an echo of thunder rolls down into the valley. What? Rain? It's still sunny up here! Then skies begin to darken, clouds thicken and advancing breezes tickle the topmost branches of the cedars. Soon I become aware of dark clouds ominously plodding toward me from the west. A flash of lightning. More thunder. I sit entranced on my deck, joyfully watching—anxiously anticipating the storm's next move. Then, like sentinels before an advancing army, the first drops of rain fall upon my deck, my head, my furry companion (he's not too sure he likes this). Then the zephyr breezes commence to flex their muscles summoning forth more lightning, more thunder. With unexpected ferocity the rain gets down to serious business—hurling its sodden ammunition upon the land; targeting stone, tree, waterway, and any unlucky critters still about. Unfazed, I remain in my deck chair enjoying the hell out of this menacing tempest as it lumbers toward me. I raise my chin, close my eyes, and revel as sharp sting of raindrops ping against my face. Kiyo begs to go inside. He's wiser than I. Suddenly the winds begin to whip the trees into a frenzy with an arctic-like, bitter vengeance. The lightening grows all-powerful, all-encompassing, threatening, and without mercy. Deafening thunder pounds against the mighty mountain's mass, ricocheting against it, rocking the cabin's ribs, reverberating against the very bones of my being. Now the rain becomes a torrent, hurtling itself angrily against the earth, cloaking all from view, like a ominous solid thing. Kiyo and I dive for the door, and safety. Me laughing. He sodden and miffed. He heads for his favorite spot behind the couch. I grab a towel, draw up a chair to the front window, and continue to monitor and marvel at the splendid antics of Mother Nature at her most grandiose and intimidating self.

Sometimes a gathering storm will prove to be a gentle thing, gracing us with only a slight whisper of rain before hurrying on quickly, as if late for a more important date East of here. But when she looses her full potential with rain so dense as to vanish the road, and all else within view—and trees so valiantly bearing her bluster, threaten to snap in two—when her deafening harbinger becomes one long continuous peel, and her lightning illuminates the entire firmament and all that lies beneath it—those are the storms that nourish some perverse corner of my psyche. (It's a family thing) Occasionally I'm treated to distant storms, spanning across the sky 50 miles north of me, above Coeur d'Alene. Those behemoths stage a light show surpassing any 4th of July firework's display. Blinding flashes of lightening leap from cloud to ground, or stunningly arch from thunderhead to thunderhead. Oh, it's these storms of the night that fuel my spirit, renewing my resolve to abide here at the top of my mountain at Chez Walden.

"For many years I was self-appointed inspector of snowstorms and rainstorms, and did my duty faithfully, though I never received one cent for it."
—Henry David Thoreau

Art Created by My Sister Bess Cornett.

Winter—I've Got You in My Sights.

I've decided that my snowmobile—heavy, and prone to getting stuck in deep snow—may not be the vehicle I really need to access my cabin during all the tough Winters to come—especially if no one is available to keep the trail packed. I have been contemplating the purchase of a side by side machine, a UTV (Utility Terrain Vehicle) with tracks that will float on top of the snow. This would make my traveling so much easier—no more pullin' and tuggin' to drag that heavy-weight out of a snowbank. A side by side will also provide more space for hauling supplies and equipment up and down the mountain—with enough power left over to tow the dogsled behind it. If this all comes to fruition I will split the dogsled in half lengthwise, widening it by a foot, and screw on plywood sides to keep loads stable. This will be so much better suited for hauling supplies *and* prevent tipping. I'm guessing Kiyo might like it better too. Not as loud as the snowmobile.

While holding onto all these lofty thoughts about a classier, more efficient snow machine I loaded up the old snowmobile onto my pickup and drove it into town. Because it had been sitting—unused—with the carburetors full of gas, it needed some professional help. While I was at the shop I spied a used UTV machine for sale. Was I dreaming? This was exactly what I had been contemplating. Tracks instead of tires. This baby will float on top of anything 'ole Man Winter can throw at me. So after a little negotiating with the shop owner—he relating that the motor had just been rebuilt and new axles installed—the price we dickered, on plus the old snowmobile, was such that I could manage and I plunked down a deposit on it.

It will soon be mine—and hopefully before the snow flies next winter.

30

> "Sometimes all you can do is not to think,
> not wonder, not imagine, not obsess.
> Just breathe, and have faith that
> everything will work out for the best."
> —Author unknown

July—and life throws me, yet again, another curve. On July 4th my sister called to tell me our Dad, who lives in North Carolina, had suffered a massive stroke. Shit! Luckily for me Nick just happened to have a load heading that way. I grabbed it—and was out there with my Dad within a week. Sister Bess flew up from Florida and together we shared hotel accommodations. (Mind you—this was the longest we had been together without doing each other bodily harm since we were kids.) We stayed there for a week, visiting Dad—buoying up his wife—and assuring us all that he was in the right place, and getting the very best care available. His wife was stressed and juggling a lot on her plate—a job—a health-care facility that was an hour's drive away—a husband that may never walk again—and keeping alive a beloved, but infirmed, old dog that Dad adores and begs to see. He wants to come home. Their house is not equipped to support the needs of a wheel-chair-bound man, nor would his wife be able to cope with the daily physical requirements of a partially paralyzed husband.

Dad knew us, and seemed grateful we were there. We had meaningful conversations with him, and I related tales of my mountaintop retreat. I think he was proud of me.

"You know Dad. I'm only able to do this because of what I learned from you. You thought I wasn't paying attention all those years ago, when you were building and remodeling houses. Maybe it was through osmosis, or a gene you handed on down to me, but I know how to wield a pretty mean hammer—and how to measure, and saw a board just once." He smiled. I'm so glad he understood.

He's lost all feeling on his left side and it's frustrating the heck out of him. It was so disheartening to see my father in this sad condition.

The last time we visited we poured over old photos—many of him as a vibrant young Marine.

Our week was up. Dad's prognosis was somewhat encouraging, and he was slated to be moved shortly into a rehab facility. Nick called, hooking me up with a load heading back to Idaho. Bess flew home, and with Kiyo in the jump-seat I fired up the 'ole semi, and nosed her westward. Trucking being what it is I didn't make it back home 'til the last week of July. So much for my Chez Walden "plan-of-the-month."

"Sherman made the terrible discovery that men make about their fathers sooner or later...that the man before him was not an aging father but a boy, a boy much like himself, a boy who grew up and had a child of his own and, as best he could, out of a sense of duty and, perhaps love, adopted a role called Being a Father so that his child would have something mythical and infinitely important: a Protector, who would keep a lid on all the chaotic and catastrophic possibilities of life."
—Tom Wolfe, *The Bonfire of the Vanities*

What the Heck?

Sometimes it feels like I'm running a chipmunk ranch up here. Beside the two-dozen or so cheeky little critters living in my wood piles there seems to be hundreds more in the piles of brush and undergrowth near the cabin. They sense full well I mean them no harm so are very daring when I'm out and about the grounds and scurry fearlessly across my deck—even while I am sitting out on it. Very often they will approach the open cabin door as though seeking more peanuts. I'm reminded of Pavlov's dogs. Kiyo, for the most part, ignores them—finding their antics tiresome and boring. He may lift his head briefly as they scurry past his nose, but in his world they don't rate a single woof. I enjoy the heck out of their sassy exploits and impudent beggings so I continue to spend my hard-earned cash on bags of peanuts to appease them. With some luck they'll stick around and continue to entertain me into the fall. They are far better "house guests" than the mice I have been trying to evict since last winter.

Impudent Little Creatures.

Henry D: If only you'd have had a pickup...

Now—I know full well that Thoreau advocated the simple live—which is why I'm attempting to follow in his footsteps. But just for a minute Henry D, imagine what more you might have accomplished on Walden Pond if only you'd had access to a faithful old pickup truck. What could be simpler? There are a multitude of things an old pickup can do for you: haul in a hefty load of stones to build a chimney—or fashion a hearth; or lug in a cord of wood for the fireplace—not one armload at a time—but a half cord at a single whack; or deliver any matter of building material right to your cabin door. Supplies that could have taken days to tote in on foot, can be delivered in the bed of a faithful 'ole pickup in one fell swoop. And if your four-wheeled baby had come equipped with a four-wheel drive you could have delved into the vast, uncharted territory about you—all those roads "less traveled by." Henry D, without my faithful four-wheeled companion I would never have attempted to follow in your footsteps. She has served me well (with just a couple of minor breakdowns) for everything from dragging downed logs off the side of the road, to hauling up the old 'buxom' Agatha. I believe Henry D—if you lived in this century—and had access to an old pickup your journey might have taken you places you could never have imagined.

Who Knew a Mountaintop Could Get this Hot?

It's August now, and damn hot. I'm just where I want to be—at Chez Walden—and it's too damned hot to work outside. I checked with my Mom in Florida and the temperature there is exactly the same there as outside my mountaintop cabin door—97%. I'd planned to use this space of time to begin the roof project. But in this heat—on a metal roof—it would be madness. Instead I find things to do inside the cabin. I start by building a hearth for my living room stove. I've been gathering stones—of which there are a plethora here—just for this purpose. Got the base entirely stoned in and mortared, and started up the walls. With each vertical foot I must stop the process long enough to let the mortar dry and set up before advancing further upward. Slow going but it looks good so far. Rewarding work. Once this is completed I will do the same in the kitchen—laying in a hearth beneath and behind where the kitchen range will rest. Even with inside work, in this heat I have to go slow and drink plenty of water. Kiyo, wiser than I, seeks out the coolest hidey-hole in the cabin, beds down and naps. Can't say I blame him.

I don't plan to get caught up here another winter without enough firewood. Last year I agonized over it. In anticipation of the coming icy blast that hovers just around the corner, Larry and I embarked on a quest and began hauling truck-loads of logs to our sites. Luckily we can still get all we need at a good price from the same old guy who supplied us last year. With each load the sands of my anxiety slip through the hourglass like butter. (Is that a proper analogy?)

I've been rethinking that rocket stove thing. I've determined that once completed they are extremely weighty. As I have no way of knowing what the previous owner did under the floor for reinforcement (aside from ripping up the floorboards to have a look-see), I don't want to risk heaping all that additional poundage on the cabin's floor. I still believe it's a great heating solution but I'll save it for the new addition. I can reinforce the floor for that specific purpose as I build it. Meanwhile, I'm looking into a new and better stove—one that is air-tight. An engineering marvel that will run for twelve hours with just one filling.

Yeah. I'll Be Able to Sleep Through the Night.

Got another load headed for Canadian but once on my way the semi choose this particular time to have issues. I had to turn the truck around, return to the shop, and lose a few days while getting it fixed. Finally on my way, and with the promise of a good-paying return load. Though frustrating, that makes it all worth-while.

I've announced to everybody who'll listen—mostly Nick—that when I get back I'm taking the rest of the month off to work on my place.

31

One Step Forward

I know a guy—a guy with a backhoe. My buddy Jim owns a small John Deere backhoe and I have been begging him to *please* haul that baby up here and shove around some dirt that needs redistricting. Because Jim is a driver like myself, he and I aren't often in the same place at the same time, but last weekend our stars were aliened. He lives north of Coeur d'Alene so once he got the backhoe loaded on his truck he still had a bit of a haul to my place. His little four-wheel-drive pickup isn't quite as tough as mine but nevertheless he managed to navigate the mountain road toting the rig right up to my driveway. The alternative would have been to unload the machine at the bottom and drive it up. This was better. Once here he proceeded to level off the terrain behind the cabin so I will have level ground on which to plant my new addition. While I had Jim and his mighty backhoe at my disposal I also had him dig two postholes at the juncture of my driveway and the logging road. This is where I will eventually plant the posts for a gate designed to keep the curious at bay when I am not around. I'd hope we might have the time to dig a trench or two for the laying in of future water and power lines. But it was not to be. We simply ran out of daylight. Maybe next summer, before I start the addition, I can get him and his machine back up here for a day. Thanks Jim!

Jim and His Mighty Backhoe.

> "We may not arrive at our port within a calculable period, but we would preserve the true course."
> —Henry David Thoreau

Huckleberry Hounds

Huckleberry season is upon us. And I'm learning that the harvest of these tiny azure jewels is a fairly lucrative one for those so inclined to ascend the mountains of this region to gather them—and apparently my mountain harbors an abundant supply. Back where I come from—New England—I don't recall ever seeing, picking or eating huckleberries, though I understand a variety of them do grow in the northeast—and are in fact—kissin' cousin to the better known blueberry. They're a favorite food of deer, birds, rodents and bears—bears traveling great distances to nosh on them. (Beware all you pickers.) Mom says she remembers eating a piece of huckleberry pie long ago and it was delectable. I'm gonna have to get me some.

It's late in July. The berries have ripened and are ready for the plucking. Up in my neck of the woods the damn huckleberry pluckers are everywhere. These 'pluckers' ascend the mountain in early morn by every conveyance known to man: jeeps—cars—campers—motorcycles—AVTs—station wagons—motorized bicycles—UTVs—pickups—golf carts. You name it—if it has wheels and a force to propel it—it will wind its way up to the huckleberry fields, whirling tornadoes of dust in it's wake. Late evening—the parade reverses—as laden with their days' yield they descend, leaving behind trashy reminders of their trek.

Their total disregard for the mountain and its inhabitants—both human and animal—is evidenced by the maimed bodies of rabbits left dead on the roadside—victims of their race to the top. We who live up here in this utopia take great pains to avoid hitting *any* creature sharing this road with us. The litter, the empty beer cans bobbing about behind their vacating vehicles offers further evidence of their distain for our environment. Couple this with they're apparent "right" to park in the middle of the road—totally blocking it for anyone else traveling this route. On two occasions I have nearly hit one of their vehicles head-on as I negotiated around a blind corner. Before I could proceed I had to find the owner, and with as much civility as I could muster ask him to *please move your damn car!* I'll be very glad when all the berries are harvested and the 'pluckers' go away. Then the only nuisance visitors I'll have to contend with will be the seldom seen bears, and the few other various and sundry creatures that eat them. (The berries—not the "pluckers." Well, let me give that some thought.)

Now, putting all those concerns aside I have yet a greater issue with these eager entrepreneurs—that of their invasion into the realm I've come to regard as "my own personal space." My domain sits high above the winding thoroughfare and can only be approached by a long driveway. From this lofty vantage point, and the absolute *privacy* of my front porch, I can assess the wonders of Mother Nature as she spreads herself wantonly out before me—mile upon vast mile, safe in the knowledge that any approaching vehicle can readily be heard from a distance of nearly a mile. So understandably, once I step out *alone* upon this scared spot, lulled by balmy zephyrs, and wooed by woodsy-sweet perfumes, I let down my guard—so to speak—and blithely regress back to those days as a uninhibited infant—or—as I like to think of it now—my "mountain-man" alter ego. As this unconstrained creature I hold dear a certain abhorrence of attire—a disregard for all which is deemed fashionable and proper by civilized man down below.

To word it delicately, I lounge about in such manner as to take full and absolute advantage of the sun's abundant supply of vitamin D.

To word it less delicately. I hang out in the nude.

Totally bare-assed!

Now, with the onslaught of those Huckleberry Hounds, I've been forced to make certain concessions— the addition of a well-intentioned tea towel—always at the ready tucked 'neath my arse—in lieu of the more proper fig leaf—of which there seem to scarcity of in my neighborhood. The word "huckleberry" came from a mistake, according to Henry David Thoreau. He said it came from hurtleberry which was a corruption of heart-berg, or hart's berry. Hurtleberry was also called Whurtleberry and Whurtles.

My "Mountain-Man" Alter Ego.

> "When formerly I was looking about to see what I could do for a living. I thought often and seriously of picking huckleberries; that surely I could do."
> —Henry David Thoreau

Losing a Couple of Friends, but Gaining a Wind Turbine

It's September. Earnest T and Sherylee have made their final decision. They will not spend another winter up here on the mountain, and they are moving to Chili—of all places! It seems they have ex-pat (ex-patriots) friends there who are livin' the 'good life.' Wouldn't be my 'cuppa tea' but each of us must step to the music of his own drummer. I wish them nothing but the best, but I will miss them terribly. They've been my bulwark—my partners in road maintenance—my suppliers of water—my friends. (Fortunately for me, Larry and Moe have stepped in to fill that void and will now provide me with all the life-sustaining elixir I require.)

> "If a man loses pace with his companions, perhaps it is because he hears a different drummer. Let him step to the music which he hears, however measured, or far away."
> —Henry David Thoreau

While they anxiously await a buyer for their very sustainable home atop ten beautifully forested acres, preparations are in full-swing for a huge yard sale. Everything unnecessary and unpackable must go! As my luck would have it they're getting rid of a brand new 400-watt wind turbine. Never even taken out of the box. I instantly shelled out the required 400 bucks and now it's mine—all mine! I'll need a tower to mount it on, and those can cost up to $500, but *I know a guy!*—a guy who can built one for me at half that cost. My job will simply be to run the power to it, hookup the wind speed indicator, and connect its batteries to a larger power box. I think the one I have can't handle more than 200 watts. I most likely will need to purchase another converter— one that will adapt the A/C power to D/C.

When in doubt, always read the instructions.

Chasing the Solar Solution

Timing is everything. Solar panel kits just went on sale. Last year I bought one for around $200—they normally sell for $300. This year they're being offered at $150! I bought two. The panels alone usually sell for $70 apiece. This kit contains three panels, two 12-volt lights, plus the controller. This ups my supply to a total of nine panels, six lights, and three controllers, a combination that will provide a total of 130 watts on a sunny day. This will be a huge boost in maintaining adequately charged batteries. Still needed: bigger, better, and more batteries. I plan on installing three panels facing east, to catch the morning sun, and three facing west to draw from the afternoon and evening sun. The remaining three will still face toward the south. I recently reviewed an experiment performed by a college kid on this very topic—solar energy. He began by placing a certain number of solar panels at a forty-five-degree angle, on a south-facing roof. He then constructed a kind of 'tree'—attaching an equal number of panels upon this 'tree', with each panel arranged to face in a variety of angles and directions—much like the leaves on a tree. His experimentally 'tree' produced thirty-percent more electrical energy than those which he had installed in the convention mode with all panels facing south at a 45 degree angle. So much for conventional wisdom. I think it behooves me to give this matter a whole lot more thought.

> "I believe that there is a subtle magnetism in Nature, which, if we unconsciously yield to it, will direct us aright."
> —Henry David Thoreau

32

Priorities—Priorities—Priorities

Yesterday I spent a happy hour or two browsing through a warehouse overflowing with an array of awe-inspiring wood-burning stoves. These babies are engineered to perform at maximum efficiency with minimum fuel . I tried not to drool as my tongue hung out with barefaced envy and desire. I'm particular drawn to the high-end airtight models. Though their cost is reasonable, I've had to conclude that I must make do with my old stove for one more winter. There's hardly any point of acquiring a new kick-ass heater if I'm not able to get myself up to the cabin. All finances considered, weighing wants against needs, I concluded I must first finish paying off that Utility Terrain Vehicle. Once paid for it will require an additional cash outlay to equipped it with the tracks needed to assure all-winter access to the cabin. So for one more brutal season (groan) I'll just have to suck-it-up, and struggle along up with my 'ole well-meaning—but inadequate pedestal stove.

My first priority—come spring—and these heating marvels go on sale—will be to put my old gal out to pasture and replace her with one of those splendid new warm-hearted, hot-bellied ladies.

During the frigid months of winter I will work on finishing off the kitchen, and totally wrap the entire cabin with a better, thicker blanket of insulation. Couple this with an air-tight stove for next winter and I should eventually be snug as that bug in that oft-mentioned rug. Before the onslaught of this winter's wrath I will tuck more insulation deep into all the cabin's existing crevices. I don't plan to be victimized again by the Arctic blasts that ferreted their way into the cabin last year.

My goal for the completion of the kitchen is a bit complex. Each step must proceed in the correct order for all to come out as planned. First I've got to haul up all the necessary supplies: sheetrock, plastic sheeting, flooring, ceiling material—and gather more stones. Once the inner shell of the kitchen's exterior wall is totally encased with a plastic moisture barrier, the sheetrock can be nailed on. That step completed, the walls can be taped, painted and finished off, allowing for the new flooring to be laid. Then comes the kitchen hearth. (My gorgeous 'new' range, hauled in from Florida last spring, still lays in wait, bidding her time at the shop of the genius who fixed all her parts. She's far too heavy to be jockeyed around more than once, so she waits patiently at the foot of the mountain while her 'throne' is made ready.)

With the hearth stones mortared in place, dried, and stable, the slow process of constructing the stone wall that will flank her backside can begin. The whole process comes to a happy climax when—with the able assistance of a few of my most robust friends—my handsome 'new' beauty can be trucked up the mountain, and planted squarely upon her final resting place. All her vents, lines, and other various accoutrements can then be connected as she officially joins the rest of the cast at Chez Walden, and begins her new, recycled life of service.

There's a September 'feel' in the air now and the local farmers have begun to bring in their crops. The second cutting of hay is bailed, dried and sits in fields waiting their customers. The evenings are becoming cooler and I'm thinking I might have to start lighting a fire soon. Fall is definitely flexing her muscles. The urgency for more wood is upon me, but the need is not as pressing as last winter. I think I've got a handle on it this year. I do want to stock in more supplies—just in case I should get snowed in. Neighbors Larry and Moe have been a big help in this area. Once a week they head into Coeur d'Alene to load up on all their supplies. If I'm going to be away, and I leave them with a list of my needs, all will be boxed and waiting for me when I return.

As a New Englander—and an advocate of Henry David Thoreau—I'm frugal as hell! Cheap even, you might say. I buy most of my clothes at Goodwill Stores. The quality is good—sometimes even great—with many items still bearing their original tags. My money stretches for a county-mile. For fifty-bucks I can buy five pair of jeans, eight shirts, and still have change to jingle in my pocket. When you're as hard on clothes as I am—and most of us truckers are—this only makes good sense. If I wreck a pair of jeans—and that's a frequent happening—I'm only out five-bucks at most. With the cooler weather nipping at my heels, it's time I head out there on my semi-annual shopping spree. Long sleeved shirts, and long-johns are now in order. With my forty-pound weight loss, last winter's wardrobe just isn't going to do it for me. Maybe after another winter of chopping wood and I will be able to boast a still smaller wardrobe.

"Cultivate poverty like a garden herb, like sage. Do not trouble yourself much to get new things, whether clothes or friends."
  —Henry David Thoreau

The Mutt

There's a very young squirrel, with absolutely no fear of either me or Kiyo, who has joined in the fun, food, and festivities of my front porch gang. He—or she—comes within inches of where I sit, and recently—when I briefly left the front door open—wandered right inside and explored the cabin.

Could this charming critter possible be a reincarnation of that infant squirrel I raised years ago as a lad of nine? We lived in Castine, Maine at the time—the home of Maine Maritime Academy. All we 'townie kids' frequented the academy's grounds as though they were our own. I was a third grader at the time, hanging out with a few of my friends on the perimeters of the Academy's football field and accompanied, as usual, with our Great Pyrenees/St. Bernard mix, Mandy. I was about to turn homeward for the night when Mandy's nose ferreted out a tiny critter lying abandoned and forlorn in the tall grass along the edge of the ball field. It looked like a baby chipmunk. I looked about for its mother but she was nowhere in sight. The puny little infant appeared to be near death. I scooped it up and high-tailed it for home.

"Mom! Look what I found! Please make it live!" (How many mothers have heard that plea?) We emptied my sister's toy box, strewed hay in the bottom, placed in a few peanut butter crackers, and a fistful of nuts.

"That should do it," we thought.

Morning's first light revealed a baby on the brink of expiration. "Do something!" I begged.

Mom called our Vet, and based upon her description our orphan was identified as a very immature squirrel.

"He probably won't live," cautioned the Vet, "but try this: Mix up a batch of rich eggnog, warm it, and add a drop or two of brandy to it. Your daughter probably has a doll's nursing bottle—use that to feed him this formula every four hours—and keep him warm."

Together we fashioned a kind of incubator from a cardboard box—an electric heating pad—and a softly crumpled towel curled about for a 'nest.' When the first few drops of eggnog hit his tummy he latched a' hold of that bottle and sucked for all he was worth. My mom set her alarm clock for an 'every-four-hour' night-time shift.

Well—it worked. It worked so well, in fact, that "The Mutt"—as he became known—grew into the most magnificent squirrel imaginable. (No doubt it was the milk, eggs, and brandy that did it.) He—or she—flaunted a ridiculously huge bushy tail—a slick, shiny grey coat—and bright inquisitive eyes. He loved to scurried up an unsuspecting pant-leg, and ride around the house perched on Mandy's furry broad back. A time or two he even accompanied me to school. The Mutt was the hit of the schoolyard—and a bit of a neighborhood celebrity.

The time was approaching when we knew he must be eased back into his own world. We first moved him into an empty rabbit hutch, just outside the kitchen door. From this vantage he could see, and smell the enticing woods beyond. Within a few weeks we further aided his assimilation back into the wilds by leaving the hutch door open during the day. That allowed him the opportunity to venture out and begin his exploration of the beckoning world beyond—while still having access to food and safety.

As all wild creatures must—he soon reverted fully back to the wild. One evening he simply didn't return to his hutch—didn't eat the food we left out for him. After that we saw only brief glimpses of him as he scurried about doing important squirrel things. I can only hope that he found a mate, lived to a ripe old age, beget many offspring, and enthralled them with tales of brandy-laced eggnog, and the people—and dog—who raised him.

> "The squirrel that you kill in jest, dies in earnest."
> —Henry David Thoreau

Larry, Darryl and Darryl. Artwork Created by My Mom.

Things Achieved

It's now a race against time, and I've come to accept that I will never accomplish everything I had planned before the Ole Man comes barrelin' in. But at least I can tick a few items off my list—and that warms my heart—and maybe my hearth as well.

Built deck and porch

Built hearth for the primary stove

Wired entire kitchen

Purchased Utility Terrain Vehicle for reliable transportation

Purchased adequate solar paneling

Acquired a wind turbine

"Never look back unless you are planning to go that way."
—Henry David Thoreau

33

This Chapter Begs Attention

Reader's caveat: The language in this chapter may be offensive to some, however, it is authentic to the story.

> "I hope you cherish this sweet way of life, and I hope you know that it comes with a price!"
> —Lyrics by Daryl Worley from
> " I just came back from a war."

Every man, woman, and child who has ever donned the uniform of our United States, and marched off into a field of conflict, returns home with demons nipping ferociously at their heels. Some with more—some with less—some far more ferocious than others. They've returned as a different person from the one who deployed from our shores. Countless combat Veterans return home damaged by the realities of war—struggling with the residuals of the terrible burden they bore daily, the knowledge that a buddy, a comrade could be blown away in a millisecond. And the lost could be far more personal—it could be themselves turned into a pile of dust .

It should come as no great surprise that many Vets develop an "I don't give a fuck" attitude. It's a survival thing. It also should be no huge leap that many—if not most—come home with some degree of PTSD (Post Traumatic Stress Disorder).

This was brought painfully home to me recently when an unexpected phone call from an old Navy buddy, prompted an urgent meeting. We got together at a nearby bar, and within a few drinks I was witnessing the outpouring of an anguished soul.

The following exchange between my former shipmate and myself sadly illustrates the tragic reality of the returned Veteran. No names will be use here because it could be anyone of you.

I was in Coeur d'Alene, preparing my rig for another East Coast run, when I got a call from one of my Navy 'brothers'. He asked if I had time to talk.

"I got time," I told him and jumped into my pickup.

We met at a local bar in downtown Spokane. A pretty young barmaid took our drink orders, and when the drinks arrived we chatted away with meaningless small talk—until the booze kicked in. Then the real stuff began to pour forth.

"I'm lonely," he said. "Can't seem to connect with anyone anymore."

I waited. I knew his story almost by heart. His marriage—like my own—had collapsed when he returned from the Gulf. It's the legacy of so many Veterans—the residuals of serving our country.

"I just can't seem to make anything work anymore. I mean I try—but just when it seems like it's going somewhere—boom! It goes south."

His story was so much more compelling than my own. Years ago, while I was still a young guy, learning the ropes of the trucking industry, and navigating a big rig in and out of 48 states, he was serving in the first gulf war—right in middle of the 'shit.' (A term commonly used by military personnel in reference to serving in—or near—a combat zone. Everyone stationed in Iraq was 'in the shit.')

He had lost friends and brothers there.

"I'm told I behave too aggressively—then I'm told I'm not aggressive enough. How can that be?"

I knew what he meant. That desire to hold someone close—while simultaneously pushing them away for fear of losing them, is a common phenomena among combat Vets, and often the chief cause of failed marriages. One minute you have a buddy—and the next minute he's dead. It's hard to get close to anyone after that.

I made no comment—I'm just here as a sounding board, so I keep quite.

"Over there we *were* somebody. When someone said they "had your 6" (military jargon for "had your back")—they meant it. Here, nobody cares—nobody has your '6.' We're simply just another cog in someone's wheel. No one get's us. No one understands."

This is why I still drive a rig. No one is looking over my shoulder. I can pretty-much do as I please—though occasionally my 'I don't give a fuck attitude' bubbles to the surface.

"We're civilians now," I offer. "Retired and aiming to live the good life."

"Bullshit!" he barks. "Good life be damned! Look around us!" he says nodding toward the others at the bar. "Where is *my* good life? Look at those guys! They are nothing like us! And we can never be anything like them ever again!"

I can only stare down at my glass. I know he's right. Never again will we know what it's like to be truly "normal"—be fully able to communicate honestly with spouses and family. Only another Veteran 'gets' us.

"I mean—look at you! Hell, you ran off to the top of a mountain. Me, I'm so damned lost I can only submerge myself in willing broads and booze! Is that the American dream? Is that the good life?"

He continued in a voice filled with pain. "You know what I do to keep my sanity—my hold on reality? I start each day by making a list. And you know what the first thing is at the top of that list? Make your bed! My crazy/irrational self tells me that if I make my bed each morning it proves I'm still alive—still in the fight, and I'm allowed to move forward into another day."

Yeah—I know how that is. Some days it's hard for me to get out of bed too—let alone make it! But like him—if I get up—I'm still in the fight.

"We all came back with demons," I quietly say.

He laughs. "Ya, I know. Hell. Sometimes I do battle with them, and other times I just let them run amok over me."

Oh how I relate to that. The holidays are just around the corner and I can hear my demons rattling their cages—howling to be set free. But mine are nowhere near as big and nasty as his.

I'm stunned by the pain I see in his eyes as he talks on. All I can do for him is listen—which seems to be enough. For now.

"You know, life is good. The alternative sucks," I venture.

"We don't know that," he blurted out angrily, with eyes averted.

We nursed our drinks and talked on for another hour or

so—painfully dancing over, under, and around the agonizing realities he faces daily.

"Last call!" the bar-keep announced.

We stood—a quick manly hug—a fleeting look into each other eyes—a hand shake—and we headed for the door.

One last touch on the shoulder. "Please. Take care. Know that I'm here for you—*anytime* you need to talk. I don't want to see your name in the obits."

"Oh, I'll be fine," he answered flashing a cheerless smile. "Just fine."

And with that we walked through the door, turned, and we each headed in a different direction.

I hope he makes his bed tomorrow.

"Could a greater miracle take place than for us to look through each other's eyes for an instant?"
   —Henry David Thoreau

Sadly, it seems civilians must think Veterans have some sort of built-in switch—one that, with a quick flick, should erase all their demons.

How often I've heard, "Get over it already. It was a long time ago."

It would appear that these useless admonishments—ineffective though they may be—if spewed forth often enough—will facilitate a solution. Unbidden memories however, are not recorded on a disc that can be callously erased and overwritten. Only with time, understanding, and probable professional intervention will these demons grow smaller—their voices gradually quelled. For a happy few the outcome will be a return to some form of their prior 'normal' life. For far too many—the demons win.

Every single day twenty-two veterans of the Iraq and Afghanistan conflicts lose the battle with their demons. This figure released by the Department of Veterans Affairs. "Every day, 22 veterans commit suicide. That is a suicide every 65 minutes."

Founded in 2004, the Suicide Prevention for America's Veterans Act is a collaboration between Democratic Senator John Walsh of Montana and the Iraq and Afghanistan Veterans of America.

My gal Tracy says we all have demons, and though that may be true, Veterans have bigger and badder ones. They have seen more, done more, experienced more, than any non-combat-civilian could even conceive of in their worst nightmare. The images and memories they carry in their heads simply don't 'go away.' As for my demon? There's rarely a day I don't think about that Christmas morning at an airfield in Iraq—and that poor broken bastard being wheeled aboard our plane. I would gladly have changed places with him.
I was middle age. He was just a kid.

> "How do you pick up the threads of an old life? How do you go on, when in your heart, you begin to understand, there is no going back? here are some things that time cannot mend, me hurts that go too deep . . . that have taken hold."
> —J.R.R. Tolkien, from *Return of the Kings*

34

Things Finished and Unfinished

We've our first cold snap of the season. That kinda puts a rush on things up here. Last fall I was very disorganized, left many tools and equipment outside, and ultimately lost them 'til after spring thaw. This year I have more time to better prepare before the snows arrive however—this early autumn chill makes me think I'd better hustle along before 'ole Man Winter comes roaring in. Currently my entire inventory of tire chains is heaped on the ground next to the truck body—as are my jumper cables—plus numerous and sundry other odds and ends. I'll be needing them this winter and rackin' my brain to remember where I last saw them. I've got to stow them *right now* in the pickup bed.

I also have a pressing need to gather more stones for the main hearth. I ran out before I could complete the entire back-wall behind the stove. With a few more stones I can finish it up in one day. It's imperative I get that done soon so my stove can be set back in place before the *real* chill sets in.

Another job left wanting is the relocation of the truck body. I planned to jockey it closer to the cabin—shifting it just slightly so the door faces west, allowing future solar panels full access to the sun's rays. To accomplish that—a seemingly pretty straightforward task, becomes a bit of a Rube Goldberg undertaking. (Rube Goldberg is best known for a series of popular cartoons depicting complicated gadgets that perform simple tasks in indirect, and convoluted ways.)

First, the woodpile must be moved, as it currently occupies the spot designated for the truck body's final resting place.

BUT, *before* the woodpile can to moved to *its'* final resting place i.e.:—the new porch.

The roof above the porch must be completed (so there'll be no tripping over the dang wood chunks as the new roof is being assembled).

Then, every last item that's been stored in the truck's body this past year, has gotta be dragged outside, temporally stowed elsewhere, in order to sufficiently lighten this behemoth for the move to *its'* final resting place.

Finally (thank the mountain gods), *I know a guy*—with all the *right stuff—* who will make this last, and final step happen.

See what I'm dealing with? Is it just me or am I so organized—or disorganized—that every job I tackle up here must be done in some sort of convoluted chronological order?

Next summer I'll finish the uncomely thing off, and make her look real pretty-like with T1-11 siding—to emulate a board and batten facade—like an old-timey barn. No one will ever guess that she began life as an old truck body. Who knows, she may serve me yet as an stylish country guest house.

Now Comes the Roof

Hallelujah! *I know a guy!* Another of my Navy buddies has offered to give me a hand with the re-roofing project at month's end. It's a reciprocal kind of deal. I need that roof on, and tight, before snowfall—and he needs firewood. So here's the deal: he's bringing his whole family up to Chez Walden, and while he and I are working on the roof, his two teen-age boys will affect the happy solution to the firewood stash. We'll turned them loose with a couple of chainsaws—my pickup—and directions to the logging company down below. Those loggers left behind the residuals of their operations—bits and pieces too small for the mills. They are piled along the roadside and are ours for the taking. The boys, I'm told, love a challenge, and the 'manly' art of hefting large hunks of timber about—cutting, chopping and splitting it all into firebox-size pieces. His wife valiantly offered to run my kitchen and keep us fed for the weekend. I don't think she fully appreciates the feeble idiosyncrasies of my kitchen. She might be more inclined to stack cordwood once she gets a look at my rustic setup.

An Old-Fashion Roof-Raisin'

The weekend finally arrived for the roof remake. When I would be off the road, at the cabin, and several of my volunteer Navy buddies were also available. Saturday morning, at first light, Erik Langlois arrived with sons Sam, age sixteen, Marc, age fourteen and Joe—just seven, plus wife Shea—age not listed. While Shea valiantly fired up my finicky cook stove we guys, fueled by good 'ole mountain air, and a quart or two of testosterone, hefted crowbars and hammers, and climbed like monkeys over the roof. The old mismatched metal sheathing quickly gave way exposing the flaws in the structural underbelly. The air was clear, the temperature perfect, and we were all in high spirits and fine form. The job moved forward without a hitch and before long we began to detect the succulent aroma of roasting chicken wafting heavenward from the cabin. At mid-morning Earl Johnson arrived and with his added help the job moved along even quicker. The boys, each one of them, were adept with hammer and nails, and fearless when it came to climbing the steep and slippery slope.

Noontime arrived and we were rewarded with an awesome array of food spread out buffet-style, all magically prepared by Shea. Don't know if it was the company, the mountain air, or the hard work, but that meal has to count for one of the finest I've ever eaten.

After dinner the boys tackled the job of obtaining the needed firewood for their Dad.

By day's end we were beat. The south-facing roof was complete, tight, and only needing a bit of trimming up. My 'crew' left with promises to come back another weekend to complete the north-facing roof. Great day. Great friends. And one more job to cross off my to-do list.

The Old Roof Was No Match for this Crew.

In Conclusion

"The tops of mountains are among the unfinished parts of the globe, whither it is a slight insult to the gods to climb and pry into their secrets, and try their effect on our humanity. Only daring and insolent men, perchance, go there."
—Henry David Thoreau

As the sun sets over the distant ridges, bathing my world in a dream-like end-of-day glow, I loll contentedly on my deck, sipping an agreeable brew, and chuckling at the antics of my chipmunk entertainers as I toss them their evening's ration of peanuts. Kiyo—sighing deeply, with obvious distain—tries hard to ignore them—wishing them away.

Here at the top of the world I've found my peace, my serenity, a place where I can just *be*. I am concerned that I may never see the cabin finished off with all that I had planned for it. The myopathy disease that plagues me more and more will eventually render my hands incapable to do the work required. I have no regrets. It's not the completion that counts, but the doing, and in the doing to find myself. That, I have accomplished here on this mountaintop—to be at one with the world—and not fight against it. To value all that has been given to me in this lifetime, and quietly perfect the art of fully enjoying it. Too many souls never find that inner calm. I am one of the lucky ones. Thank you Henry D for mapping the trail, but answer me this Henry. Have I been insolent or daring?

Year One completed—and so my saga ends here—for now. My journey has thrust me forth into the universe and beyond. I've flirted with the cosmos and wished on the stars. Whatever I did not accomplish this year, I will do next—and keep on doing, as long as my hands can hold a tool. This is my life. I could fight it—scream to the gods of its unfairness—its inequities—or except it—keep on truckin', continually moving forward for as long as I've breath, courage, and above all, an outrageous sense of humor. To waste ones energies, talents—to tarnish an impermeable spirit—waging war against perceived injustices, can only begat a bitter existence—and an early grave.

The alternative is acceptance.

That's what I did Henry D. I did my best to walk in your footsteps.

> "The surface of the earth is soft and impressible by the feet of men; and so with the paths which the mind travels. How worn and dusty, then, must be the highways of the world, how deep the ruts of tradition and conformity! I did not wish to take a cabin passage, but rather to go before the mast and on the deck of the world, for there I could best see the moonlight amid the mountains."
> —Henry David Thoreau.

www.ingramcontent.com/pod-product-compliance
Lightning Source LLC
Chambersburg PA
CBHW040314170426
43195CB00021B/2971